STREETS

Intelligence Preparation of the Battlefield for Urban Operations

Jamison Jo Medby • Russell W. Glenn

Prepared for the United States Army

RAND | ARROYO CENTER

The research described in this report was sponsored by the United States Army under Contract No. DASW01-96-C-0003.

Library of Congress Cataloging-in-Publication Data

Medby, Jamison Jo.
    Street smart : intelligence preparation of the battlefield for urban operations /
Jamison Jo Medby, Russell W. Glenn.
        p. cm.
    "MR-1287."
    Includes bibliographical references.
    ISBN 0-8330-3171-6
    1. Urban warfare. 2. Military intelligence—United States. 3. United States.
Army—Drill and tactics. I. Glenn, Russell W. II. Title.

U167.5.S7 M44 2002
355.4'26—dc21

                                                                                    2002021364

Cover artwork by Priscilla B. Glenn
Cover design by Barbara Angell Caslon

Published 2002 by RAND
1700 Main Street, P.O. Box 2138, Santa Monica, CA 90407-2138
1200 South Hayes Street, Arlington, VA 22202-5050
201 North Craig Street, Suite 202, Pittsburgh, PA 15213
RAND URL: http://www.rand.org/
To order RAND documents or to obtain additional information,
contact Distribution Services: Telephone: (310) 451-7002;
Fax: (310) 451-6915; Email: order@rand.org

This monograph discusses how the U.S. Army's intelligence preparation of the battlefield (IPB) process should be adapted for military operations on urbanized terrain (MOUT). It notes the capabilities of this process to help a unit engage successfully in any type of operation, and it suggests modifications to the traditional process in order to address the operational and analytic difficulties posed by urbanized areas.

This study will be of interest to armed forces and intelligence community personnel planning for or conducting operations in urban areas. It will also be of interest to any armed forces, law enforcement, and intelligence community personnel with the need to assess and address the changing threat conditions emerging from urbanization.

This research was undertaken for the Assistant Secretary of the Army for Acquisition, Logistics, and Technology and was conducted in the Force Development and Technology Program of RAND Arroyo Center. The Arroyo Center is a federally funded research and development center sponsored by the United States Army.

For more information on RAND Arroyo Center, contact the Director of Operations (telephone 310-393-0411, extension 6500; FAX 310-451-6952; e-mail donnab@rand.org), or visit the Arroyo Center's Web site at http://www.rand.org/ard/.

CONTENTS

FIGURES

From the beginning of the history of conflict, gathering information about one's foe and using it against him has been a critical precept for success in war. Having superior knowledge about the terrain and weather is also a well-accepted criterion for achieving victory in battle. The armed forces of the United States have long understood these prescriptions and have amassed an array of technologies, techniques, analytic methods, and talented personnel to ensure intelligence superiority.

The emergence of new cities and the expansion of established urban hubs have challenged this intelligence superiority in many ways. Buildings and infrastructure neutralize U.S. technological advantage by stifling electronic intelligence capabilities. Urban construction imposes extreme burdens on "knowing the terrain," vastly increasing the amount of information to be considered. Buildings alter maneuver routes, change unit type and weapons use considerations, and hide personnel and equipment. Urban infrastructure, which includes utilities and public works, can impose severe restrictions on unit operations if the infrastructure is required to remain operable during the conduct of military activities. Residents of an urban area complicate situational awareness and threat identification by populating the operational area with thousands and thousands of actors who engage in constantly changing activities, and who have a variety of interests and intentions. Knowing what groups exist in an urban area, what relationships exist between them, and how each population group will respond to an activity is critical to operational success but often difficult to decipher. The combination of the increased number of people, urban construction, and urban infrastructure also hampers "knowing the enemy." Threats may be many and varied. Each threat might employ different tactics, techniques, and procedures that can be invisible because of the concealment provided by urban construction.

Regardless of these detrimental effects, the ubiquity of urbanization today ensures that the U.S. Army will be called upon to operate in villages, towns, and cities. Adversaries may also draw U.S. forces into urban areas in order to neutralize American technological capabilities. If the Army is to remain superior in all types of engagements, it must overcome both the operational and analytic challenges that cities produce. The service is currently addressing these problems with more sophisticated intelligence equipment and a lighter, more technologically advanced force. Yet there is already a tool available that can assist in both the planning and the execution of operations and intelligence missions in urban areas. The tool is intelligence preparation of the battlefield (IPB).

IPB is an analytic process used to organize and analyze information on terrain, weather, and the threat within a unit's area of operations and associated area of interest. Through its systematic four-step approach, members of command and intelligence staffs use IPB to predict how an adversary will act within a certain area of operations (AO) given the terrain, weather, and other contextual conditions. IPB also helps in developing a collection plan that best suits mission needs. Because it is a tool of the mind, IPB can be adapted to any operation for any size force. It is comprehensive enough to manage the seemingly overwhelming amounts of information coming from many sources. It is also immediately available; it does not require the deployment of sophisticated equipment.

IPB is currently limited, however, in part because of entrenched ideas about the types and locations of operations the U.S. Army will conduct. Traditionally, IPB has focused on force-on-force operations against a known enemy on sparsely populated terrain. Threat and terrain analyses were therefore matters of relatively straightforward mapping of threat doctrinal formation and tactics in the area of operations.

IPB for urbanized areas is not so clear-cut. Terrain analysis must include both the terrain on which the city sits and a comprehensive assessment of how buildings will affect maneuver, weapons systems, logistics, and all battlefield operating systems (BOS). Civilians on the battlefield add a crucial dimension to the analysis, requiring thoughtful consideration of all of their many potential effects. Some of these implications include the following:

- The presence of civilians affects movement and maneuver.

- The presence of soldiers among a foreign population requires a more thorough study of demographics and cultures in order to maintain mission legitimacy.

- Audiences within and beyond the AO, watching military activities within it, need to be understood if information campaigns are to succeed.

- The number and variety of people within an urban AO might blur threat identification.

- Civilians wittingly or unwittingly help an adversary achieve its goals.

All of these considerations, and many more, force population considerations to come to the analytic foreground. Importantly, analysis must include cultural intelligence in a more thorough approach to threat evaluation. The resulting assessment will help determine how each subsector of a population might present potential benefits or threats to the friendly force or hinder or provide assistance to the adversary. This assessment will also help to make the course-of-action development that results from IPB more robust. The traditional action-reaction-counteraction approach to COA development may not encompass the higher-order effects that result from an action because of the interconnectedness of urban surroundings. Peripheral and unanticipated outcomes of any action undertaken by the friendly or adversarial force in an urban area must be forecast and included in IPB in order to mitigate unintended effects.

With the original goals of IPB in mind—to decipher the effects of the terrain, weather, and threat in order to predict how the enemy will act to help the commander select the best course of action for the friendly unit—in this monograph we propose methods to overcome the difficulties caused by urbanization. We note that there is a vast number of tools and technologies already in place to assist in conducting IPB, the Marine Corps *Generic Intelligence Requirements Handbooks* and the methods proposed in Army Field Manual (FM) 34-130 being the most prominent. The methods and tools presented here are not meant to usurp existing doctrine or methods already in place. Rather, the ideas presented are intended to help intelligence and command staffs adapt the tools they already have available as well as to present new tools that can be selected depending on the job to be done. Not all of the tools presented are necessary or relevant to every operation. Each can be used independently depending on the needs of the commander and his staff. Many are presented in a very simplified format (e.g., the information analysis matrix and perception analysis matrix) to ensure that any unit, regardless of its size or technological capabilities, can still use them. These tools might also provide a starting point for intelligence professionals working on automating intelligence efforts. They are suggested as methods that can be used independently or together to assist the commander and his staff effectively plan for the mission ahead.

ORGANIZATION OF THIS MONOGRAPH

Following the introduction, each chapter of this work is devoted to IPB and how it can be modified for MOUT (military operations on urbanized terrain). Chapter Two provides an overview of current doctrinal IPB. It briefly describes the procedure's four steps and the tasks, purposes, and intent associated with each. The end of this chapter includes a discussion of why slightly modifying the names of each of the steps of IPB might be a useful first step in adapting the process to better address urban dilemmas and future operational challenges. It should be noted that the term *intelligence preparation of the battlefield* might also appear dated and out of synch with today's realities in the field. It may be inappropriate to think of an operational area as a "battlefield" during stability missions, support missions, disaster relief scenarios, and especially when undertaking homeland security operations. The term IPB itself is not changed within this document, however, in order to maintain clarity and consistency with current doctrine. Perhaps at some point the Army should consider renaming the process to better correlate with the other services—converting the name to *intelligence preparation for the battlespace,* for instance. An even more appropriate moniker might be the one already used by law enforcement agencies within the United States: *intelligence preparation for operations.*

Chapter Three describes the dilemmas posed by urban terrain. A city's challenges are described in terms of the features that define the built-up area, namely, the underlying terrain, buildings, infrastructure and people. This chapter is not an exhaustive delineation of the difficulties pertaining to urban terrain. Rather, it provides an overview of the potential problems that might appear in a city during any type of operation. Every city and every operation is unique. The categories used to define the problems presented by urban operations can help the commander and his staff ensure that each type of problem is addressed during mission planning.

Chapter Four considers step one of IPB, which current doctrine calls *define the battlefield area.* It describes how the concepts of METT-TC (mission, enemy, terrain, troops, time available, and civilians) and TTP (tactics, techniques, and procedures) can be used to help define the area of operations (AO) and more appropriately delineate the corresponding area of interest (AOI) and battlespace. It incorporates ideas on how urban AOI and battlespaces might fundamentally differ from the areas outlined for operations undertaken in open terrain. For instance, infrastructure such as electricity, banking capabilities, and media that connect a city to far-flung areas might often be nodes of interest or influence that are not adjacent to the AO. Ensuring that these areas are considered during all phases of any type of urban operation is driven by the idea that they are an integral part of the AOI and battlespace.

Chapter Five describes modifications to IPB step two, doctrinally entitled *describe the battlefield's effects.* It includes discussion of urban terrain and weather analysis—areas already thoroughly investigated by the Army and Marine Corps. It also takes a possibly controversial step by suggesting that population analysis—which in this work includes demographic analysis, cultural intelligence, media analysis, and non-U.S. actor considerations (other than threats)— should be of central concern to staffs working in urban areas. As part of this discussion, we review tools and ideas already used to analyze the population; most are derived from current doctrine (particularly SASO and PSYOP doctrine) and from the Center for Army Lessons Learned (CALL). The authors also propose what are thought to be newly introduced ideas such as *perception analysis,* in an effort to demonstrate that people in urban areas can affect any aspect of a given mission and thus require a great deal of attention during analysis and mission planning. The chapter describes a city's population as a variety of subgroups, each requiring individual attention as an operation unfolds. It is proposed that an investigation of the relationships among these subpopulations might identify critical points within the population that can be shaped to help achieve mission success. The chapter also includes a discussion of how a city's infrastructure (utilities and public facilities) can affect operations. How is the infrastructure used for sustaining a city's population? How can it be used as a weapon or weapons platform in urban campaigns? These and other questions are addressed in this chapter's discussion of IPB step two.

Chapter Six is dedicated to reconsidering the components of IPB step three, doctrinally known as *evaluate the threat.* The authors first suggest that urban populations confuse threat identification by populating the operating area with a variety of known and unknown challenges to a mission. The presence of a multitude of possible threats requires modification of the current doctrinal method employed in IPB step three, which traditionally instructs analysts to evaluate only a known adversary based on the assumption that its doctrine and tactics are known. The authors suggest a method of first *identifying* and then *defining a threat based on its own interests, intentions, capabilities, and the vulnerabilities of the friendly unit.* A definition of threat is provided (current doctrine does not have one), along with ways to use this definition to evaluate the nature of each population group (identified and parsed using the methods introduced for conducting step two of IPB, as discussed in Chapter Five). The *continuum of relative interests* is introduced as a tool to help manage information on each population group and evaluate how each group can affect an operation. Using the continuum, each population group's capabilities, interests, and intentions can be constantly measured in relation to mission requirements. This chapter concludes with a nonexhaustive compilation of the most common adversarial urban tactics gleaned from a variety of lessons-learned sources.

IPB step four, *develop enemy courses of action,* is the subject of Chapter Seven. This chapter principally demonstrates how a known method of intelligence, the *analysis of competing hypotheses,* can be used to better determine adversary courses of action. It demonstrates that rather than trying to confirm a proposed COA, analysts should attempt to disconfirm potential alternatives. By viewing the proposed COA in this way, named area of interest and target area of interest selection become especially critical. The chapter also posits methods for anticipating and evaluating the peripheral effects and indirect outcomes of urban events. It incorporates the *continuum of relative interests* to help predict how population groups might react to changing conditions within the operational area, how the infrastructure (or lack of it) might affect immediate aspects of the operation as well as its less immediate effects, or how an act by a single soldier might affect the overall operation. In effect, we propose some preliminary ways to predict and depict the "snowball" effect of any action taken within the operational area.

Finally, this report draws conclusions on how current IPB doctrine can be modified to better suit urban operations. Urban populations are a primary concern in MOUT that warrant significant analytic effort. Technology devoted to addressing the need to gather and analyze the huge amount of information that comes from urban operations is also recommended; specific recommendations in this regard are the subject of a future study. In addition, doctrinal deficiencies that are identified throughout the text are reiterated, along with suggestions on how to correct them.

Overall, the authors suggest that IPB is a sound methodology for assessing the characteristics of an urban operational area. With modifications that allow it to more flexibly assimilate information about urban population groups, construction, and infrastructure, IPB can provide intelligence that the process as it is currently employed cannot supply. In short, superior knowledge of the terrain, weather, and threat can be gained and maintained by using IPB methods with adaptations that allow it to more thoroughly address urban issues.

ACKNOWLEDGMENTS

We are grateful to a number of individuals for their advice and assistance with this monograph. Major Howard Nichol (British Army), Captain Steven Fomiatti (Australian Army), Major John Crump (USA, retired), Major Wayne Barefoot, and Captain Ron Martin, all instructors at the Army Intelligence School, consistently went out of their way to provide knowledge on current U.S. doctrine and procedures. Their real-world experiences also provided valuable insights into how doctrine is applied in deployments. Mr. Mike Ley and Captain Jeanne Lang of Fort Huachuca's intelligence doctrine division kept us informed of changes to existing doctrine and formulations of emerging viewpoints. Mike also tirelessly provided answers to a myriad of technical, doctrinal, and tactical questions. Brian Jenkins provided insightful guidance on the threat analysis portion of the work. Thanks to General Ron Christmas (USA, retired), Mr. John Gordon, Major Scott Crino, and Mr. Patrick Bogue for reviewing this document and offering valuable suggestions on how it could be improved. A special thank you for Major General Jim Delk (USA, retired), who went out of his way to carefully review the draft and provide well-considered critiques and contributions.

The members of RAND's Urban Operation team—most notably Scott Gerwehr—provided input and advice at every stage of the writing process. Special thanks goes to everyone in the 304th MI Battalion, Company A, Class 99-5 (Squad 1 in particular).

ABBREVIATIONS

AA	Avenue of Approach
ACH	Analysis of Competing Hypothesis
AO	Area of Operations
AOI	Area of Interest
AOR	Area of Responsibility
BDA	Battle Damage Assessment
BOS	Battlefield Operating System
C2	Command and Control
CA	Civil Affairs
CALL	Center for Army Lessons Learned
CCIR	Commander's Critical Information Requirements
COA	Course of Action
COG	Center of Gravity
EEFI	Essential Elements of Friendly Information
FFIR	Friendly Force Information Requirements
FM	Field Manual
FMSO	Foreign Military Studies Office
G2	The intelligence section of a unit, battalion and above

GIRH	Generic Information Requirements Handbook
HC	Host City
HN	Host Nation
HPT	High-Payoff Target
HUMINT	Human Intelligence
HVT	High-Value Target
IFOR	Implementation Force
IO	Information Operations
IPB	Intelligence Preparation of the Battlefield
IR	Intelligence Requirement
IRA	Irish Republican Army
J2	Section on a joint staff responsible for intelligence operations
JP	Joint Publication
LOC	Line of Communication
LOS	Line of Sight
MCIA	Marine Corps Intelligence Activity
MCRP	Marine Corps Reference Publication
MCWP	Marine Corps Warfighting Publication
MDMP	Military Decisionmaking Process
METT-TC	Mission, Enemy, Terrain, Troops, Time Available, and Civilians
MOOTW	Military Operations Other Than War
MOUT	Military Operations on Urbanized Terrain
NAI	Named Area of Interest
NGO	Nongovernmental Organization
OB	Order of Battle

OCOKA	Observation and Fields of Fires, Concealment and Cover, Obstacles, Key Terrain, and Avenues of Approach
PA	Public Affairs
PIR	Priority Intelligence Requirement
PSYOP	Psychological Operations
PVO	Private Volunteer Organization
R&S	Reconnaissance and Surveillance
ROE	Rules of Engagement
RPG	Rocket-Propelled Grenade
RUC	Royal Ulster Constabulary
S2	The intelligence section of a unit, brigade and below
SA	Situational Awareness
SASO	Stability and Support Operation
TTP	Tactics, Techniques, and Procedures
UN	United Nations
U.S.	United States
USAIC & FH	United States Army Intelligence Center and Fort Huachuca
USMC	United States Marine Corps

Chapter One

INTRODUCTION

Know the enemy, know yourself; your victory will never be endangered.
Know the ground, know the weather; your victory will then be total.

Sun Tzu
The Art of War

Information superiority: The capability to collect, process, and disseminate an uninterrupted flow of information while exploiting or denying an adversary's ability to do the same; [when] there are no clearly defined adversaries [information superiority is] when friendly forces have the information necessary to achieve operational objectives.

Decision superiority: Better decisions arrived at and implemented faster than an opponent can react, or in a noncombat situation, at a tempo that allows the force to shape the situation or react to changes and accomplish its mission.

Joint Vision 2020

Men, women, and children awoke from a night's rest and began their day with no thought that it might be their last, or so it was for those who suffered from the dreadful disease in the first days.[1] Seemingly

---

[1]This summary of the London cholera epidemic relied on several sources, including "Cholera," *http://www.biology.lsa.umich.edu/courses/bio118/cholera.htm;* G.L. Gilbert, "From Broad St. to Prospect via Milwaukee: Water Contamination and Human Disease," *http://www.usyd.edu.au/~cidm/page/inoculum/water.htm;* and material from the UCLA John Snow web site, in particular Ralph R. Frerichs, "History, Maps and the Internet: UCLA's John Snow Site," *http://www.ph.ucla.edu/epi/snow.html.* Figure 1.1 is from the UCLA web site *http://www.ph.ucla.edu/epi/snow/snowmap1c_1854.html.*

1

perfectly healthy at dawn, within hours the victims' eyes and cheeks would sink into their faces. Pinching skin would leave the flesh malformed for too long a time. Diarrhea struck suddenly, so severe that the body could lose a fifth of its weight in a single day. Within twelve hours the disease could kill what a half-day before was a carefree child, loving mother, or the father on whose wages the family's welfare depended. It was 1854 in London, and Asiatic cholera was ravaging the city.

The cause of the disease and how it was transmitted were points of debate at the time. Many believed it was borne in *miasmata,* gases from swamps or decayed organic matter. Others, Dr. John Snow included, thought it was instead caused by an infectious microbe. Snow lived in Soho, an area particularly hard hit by the outbreak. The doctor himself wrote in 1854 that

> the most terrible outbreak of cholera which ever occurred in this kingdom is probably that which took place in Broad Street, Golden Square, and the adjoining streets a few weeks ago. Within two hundred and fifty yards of the spot where Cambridge Street joins Broad Street, there were upwards of five hundred fatal attacks of cholera in ten days. . . . The mortality in this limited area probably equals any that was ever caused in country, even by the plague, and it was more sudden, as the greater number of cases terminated in a few hours.[2]

Snow realized that most of the Soho cases were people living or working within a part of the neighborhood drawing water from the Broad Street pump; 79 of the 89 people who died in the first week of the local outbreak lived near or regularly acquired water from that source. He determined that at least eight of the remaining ten had drunk water from it shortly before they died. Cholera rates were lower in a nearby workhouse that had its own pump and in a local brewery where a considerable number of employees chose alternative refreshment. Dr. Snow took his findings to the Board of Guardians of St. James's parish, the political organization responsible for the area's welfare; the board directed the removal of the Broad Street pump handle the following day. Snow later demonstrated his

---

[2]Ralph R. Frerichs, "History, Maps and the Internet: UCLA's John Snow Site," *http://www.ph.ucla.edu/epi/snow.html,* p. 4.

analysis using the map shown in Figure 1.1. Each dash (some so densely packed as to appear solid columns) represents a cholera death at that address. The clustering around the Broad Street pump is obvious.

It is not possible to definitively credit Dr. Snow's efforts with the ending of the local cholera epidemic. The number of fatalities was declining even before the removal of the handle, in no small part because three-quarters of the area's residents had by that time fled the

RANDMR1287-1.1

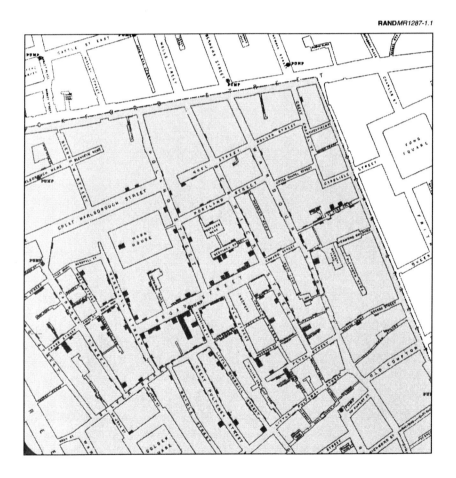

Figure 1.1—Broad Street Area Cholera Cases

neighborhood. Substantial evidence nevertheless points to his having determined the source of the problem; his actions were likely significant in ending the disaster. They were also influential in drawing attention to other epidemic-related work he was performing during the same period. Snow studied the number of cholera deaths among a population of 300,000 Londoners served by two water suppliers (the Lambeth Company and Southwark and Vauxhall Company). Those residents supplied by the Lambeth Company, which collected its water upriver of London and thereby provided water nearly free of the city's sewage and many other contaminants, had a rate of cholera deaths one-tenth that of the Southwark and Vauxhall Company, whose River Thames water was more polluted.

Snow understood the importance of collecting relevant information on London's natural terrain (river), population (numbers of cholera cases), and infrastructure (water supply companies and pumps) in finding solutions to the challenges that confronted him. His later visual presentation of the data backing his Broad Street analysis demonstrates that his was the same kind of thinking that today's military analysts will need to employ during contemporary urban operations worldwide.

Snow's work demonstrates that being able to understand and depict the patterns and interconnections of terrain, infrastructure, and populations can help establish the root cause of an urban dilemma, a critical skill for any military commander or staff member who will face similarly problematic situations in cities to which they are deployed. In addition to understanding the operational context of a mission, participants in conflicts must obtain critical information about their surroundings and adversaries while shielding their own capabilities from the eyes of the enemy. Sun Tzu articulated this idea over two thousand years ago. In modern American military parlance, this idea is equivalent to gaining *information superiority* and converting this information into usable material—intelligence—to assist a commander in gaining *decision superiority*.

American armed forces seemingly have the technology, tools, and personnel available to achieve decision superiority in any operation. For example, large investments are made in mapping, reconnaissance and surveillance equipment, and aerial photography technology. The increasing urbanization of the globe, however, shaves the

U.S. margin of information supremacy because cities have unique characteristics that complicate information gathering and the military operations the information is intended to support. Buildings and infrastructure tend to degrade the capability of imaging and communication equipment. Urban infrastructure, including electricity, media, satellites, and other resources, increase the capabilities and numbers of people producing, sharing, and receiving information via television, Internet, telecommunications, and radio. The masses of people in an urban area simultaneously provide more sources of information in the form of HUMINT (human intelligence) and act to overwhelm the collection and analysis that all-source intelligence can provide. The sheer density and diversity of all features of an urban area—buildings, infrastructure, people—flood extant technologies in ways that often make information superiority unreachable.

The degradation in the ability to collect information is exacerbated by the tremendous volume of information that at first look appears necessary to gather and analyze. For instance, buildings are constructed from a variety of materials, stand at inconsistent heights, and serve a variety of functions. Noting the location, ownership, and density of a city's construction is therefore essential for any type of urban operation, combat or noncombat. Urban infrastructure, such as electrical lines, water mains, and telephone wires, can be a tool of both ground and information warfare; it must also be maintained in order to fulfill the needs of the city's residents and friendly forces both during and after operations. Additionally, the cultural characteristics of a foreign city can be quite different from anything with which a soldier is familiar. These characteristics must be identified, analyzed, and appropriately described in order to establish situational awareness and develop appropriate rules of engagement (ROE). Sectors and subsectors of the city's population can affect friendly operations in a variety of ways. They can hinder or help a unit's accomplishment of its mission. Being able to distinguish which groups fulfill either of these functions is therefore critical to the successful conduct of the operation. Determining which groups or individuals pose the greatest threat (or even a slight one) requires a thorough analysis of the demographics and culture of a city, a requirement of considerable scale in today's metropolitan amalgamations.

Managing all of the information required for completing an intelligence picture is a daunting task for a staff, especially given the collection and analysis difficulties introduced by an urban landscape. Fortunately, there is an intelligence tool already used by the Army that can help sort and assess information and identify gaps in available information. This technique is **intelligence preparation of the battlefield (IPB)**. IPB is a four-step, cyclical process that produces intelligence pictures of the enemy, terrain, and weather within a designated area of operations (AO) and its associated area of interest (AOI). Each step of IPB provides a means of putting Sun Tzu's axiom and the corresponding Defense Department definitions into practice. It helps a commander to better "know his enemy" by providing guidelines on the type of information to collect about the adversary's force structure, doctrine, tactics, and leadership. The IPB process provides the organization and methods of collecting, defining, and analyzing information in order to "know the ground" and "know the weather" to determine how enemy and friendly operations will be affected by each in the designated area.

Although it is not the "silver bullet" that can ensure decision superiority or even information superiority, IPB can begin to manage the diversity and density of information prevalent in urban areas. It can also be a critical tool of collection management, helping to ensure that intelligence requirements are as specific and relevant as possible to the operation. The process of IPB can also be used as a logical starting point for developing new technologies to help address the infinite information-collection and analysis dilemmas that urban areas pose to any military operation.[3]

As a methodology for managing information in a complex context, IPB is well suited for urban operations. But the tools traditionally used to conduct the IPB process have not kept pace with the varying types of operations and adversaries the Army encounters. Enemies, battlefields, and operations are different from what is traditionally envisioned. As the brief description of a city's inherent dilemmas has

---

[3]A discussion of the types of technologies that are currently in use or can be hypothesized for achieving information superiority and decision superiority in urban operations is well beyond the scope of this report. However, the statement is included herein so readers can begin to generate ideas on how these goals should be achieved, using IPB as a framework.

already pointed out, the complexity of a city requires a thorough and flexible approach to intelligence collection, integration, and analysis. IPB is capable of handling these dilemmas with some modifications. Those modifications, which will help IPB to be better suited for urban operations, are the subject of this work. Some of the topics that will be discussed include the following:

- Traditional terrain analysis should include a comprehensive assessment of urban construction. What materials are used? What are the designs and dimensions? Is there an apparent plan to the city, or is building more haphazard?

- IPB should include investigation of urban infrastructure. What are its components? Who supports it and who is supported by it? What is necessary to sustain the population?

- A study of populations including demographic details, cultural norms, and perceptions should be incorporated in order to understand the indigenous culture. This is particularly true for the information operation component of any mission.

- Population subgroups might pose a variety of different threats for a friendly unit. Threat identification must therefore precede threat evaluation. By developing cultural intelligence, groups and individual members of a population can be identified as threatening, nonthreatening, somewhere in between, or even both. Given the vast number of subpopulations that exist in any urban area, this identification process is a necessary step prior to determining the capabilities and activities of a threat.

- Following the identification of urban adversaries (individuals or groups found to be most threatening to the friendly force), their capabilities must be evaluated in terms of how buildings, public utilities, infrastructure, and the city's residents can be used as part of their dynamic arsenal. Courses of action (COAs) developed for the adversary must include all of these elements.

- The variety of population groups resident in a city requires the development of individual COAs. Because each population group might influence the actions of the friendly or adversarial unit, it is necessary to consider how they might do so.

- COA development for both friendly and adversarial forces must also include how the actions undertaken by one element identified in an operational area can affect a number of other elements or actions within the same area, or even beyond it; meaning that the interconnectedness of an urban area produces intentional and unintentional consequences for every act, and the commander and his staff must be aware of them all. To illustrate, consider a disregard for the laws of land warfare that precipitates the intentional destruction of a mosque within a zone monitored by an international coalition of soldiers. The reaction of that segment of the population served by the mosque may lead to extensive media coverage, or it could lead to physical attacks on the coalition force if they are somehow implicated in its destruction. Assessing the potential for these types of outcomes, from the strategic, operational, and tactical perspectives, is critical for the overall success of the unit's mission.

- In addition to identifying "ground truth," IPB must address matters of perception. Each step of the IPB process should include questions about the public's assessment of ongoing events to ensure that friendly force activities are being interpreted as intended. How extant populations perceive activities of the adversarial force should also be monitored. Information operations can influence public opinion in a variety of ways. They are only effective, however, if a population's culture and perceptions are sufficiently understood. Friendly force perceptions and analytic bias among the intelligence staff must also be considered.

Ideas about how to adapt IPB to urban operations, like those listed above, are the focal point of this work. These thoughts are not meant to replace existing doctrine. Rather, they are intended to spur further discussion and promote an exchange of ideas on the most pressing problems of conducting IPB for urban operations.

The reader will note that there are some suggested modifications to doctrinal labels presented in this work. These modifications are intended to unlock the current force-on-force mindset and expand thinking about IPB beyond a sterile battlefield. It is hoped that the small modifications will help staffs understand the very different dilemmas that might be present in disaster relief or peacekeeping operations where a battlefield does not necessarily exist. These labels are not meant to replace existing doctrine.

New ideas and methods are introduced. For instance, the *continuum of relative interests* is presented as part of a more complete threat evaluation process that first seeks to identify the most threatening elements in the AO and AOI. Construction of the continuum, as will be described, seeks to evaluate the capabilities, interests, and intentions of each relevant population group and then compare them to the vulnerabilities of the friendly force. The *analyses of competing hypotheses* (ACH) technique, presented as a tool to evaluate enemy courses of action, is currently used by many intelligence analysts but is not yet incorporated into formal doctrine. This approach is intended to promote a new way to look at predicting enemy courses of action.

Urban applications of existing IPB concepts are also discussed. Descriptive overlays and pattern and link analysis products are all described, for example. It is hoped that by presenting them here, analysts who are unfamiliar with the resources currently available will gain an appreciation for the variety of analytic tools that can improve the IPB process during any urban operation.

It is important to note that the authors do not envision that the tools presented herein can or will be used for every type of operation for every size unit. Small units will not have the personnel or time to conduct some of the analyses discussed. The type of operation will definitely affect the specific type of tool used. It is hoped that staffs conducting IPB use the ideas presented as options to consider when completing the planning process, to use them as they see fit for the mission being conducted.

Equally important to mention is the method of presentation of the material. This work is presented as a set of ideas. The ideas are not specific to the changes in force structure being undertaken at the time of writing. Nor are they specifically designed to work with existing intelligence or planning technology, although these criteria were definitely considered when preparing this monograph. The presentation of ideas that are not associated with a single technology or structural change is deliberate. IPB is a process based on ideas. Analysis is driven by thought; technology merely enhances the capability to share information and thought. The technology that can improve IPB and the planning process deserves more attention than can be given in this report. It is believed that the information included herein will be valuable to the intelligence staffs of current and future units, regardless of their size or level of technology.

One last caveat is warranted. It is understood that IPB, as currently written and practiced, is primarily an intelligence function dedicated to understanding the context of an operation and describing the threat to a mission. Throughout the text, however, the authors take the approach that IPB is also married to operational thought and planning. As a result, some of the discussions included often concern friendly force operations and courses of action. For example, there are sections devoted to perception management and friendly force vulnerability assessment that take a decidedly operational edge. Some of the overlays listed in Chapter Five are more suited for tactical planning than intelligence depiction. These discussions, and others like them that sometimes blur the line between operations and intelligence, are included to emphasize the belief that IPB truly should be a collaborative effort of the operations and intelligence teams.

Chapter Two

INTELLIGENCE PREPARATION OF THE BATTLEFIELD: AN OVERVIEW

We expect a great deal from intelligence. We ask intelligence to describe in detail places we have never seen, to identify customs and attitudes of societies fundamentally different from our own, to assess the capabilities of unique and unfamiliar military or paramilitary forces and to forecast how these societies and forces will act in the future. Most notably, we want intelligence to enter the thought process of an enemy commander and predict, with certainty, what course of action he intends to pursue, possibly even before he knows himself what he is going to do.

Marine Corps Doctrinal Publication 2: *Intelligence*

Intelligence preparation of the battlefield (IPB) is the Army's method for collecting, organizing, and processing intelligence. It is an analytic framework for organizing information to help provide timely, accurate, and relevant intelligence to the military decision-making process (MDMP) (see Figure 2.1). The intent of IPB is to give the commander and his staff information on the conditions within his operational area—comprising the area of operations, area of interest, and battlespace—that could affect the outcome of his mission. Conditions to be identified include the relevant characteristics of the weather, terrain, population groups and subgroups, media, and infrastructure. IPB also provides a method of gathering information to describe how each of these relevant characteristics influences the friendly unit, enemy unit (if applicable), and the other players in the operational area. IPB is critical to timely, accurate decisionmaking.

A key component of IPB is identifying, evaluating, and describing the threat(s) to a unit's mission. Although the definition of threat is often mission dependent (e.g., the threat to a flood relief mission may be

11

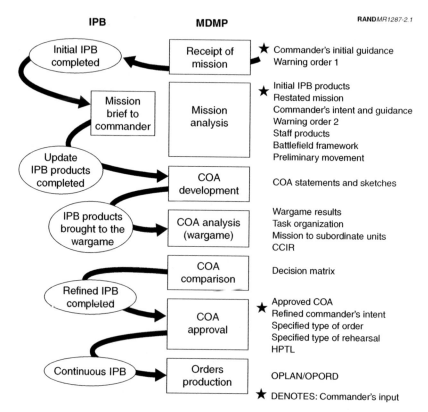

SOURCE: FM 34-130/MCRP 2-12A, *Intelligence Preparation of the Battlefield (Initial Draft),* Washington D.C.: Department of the Army, 1999, p. 1-2.

Figure 2.1—IPB and the MDMP

the lack of helicopter landing spots; in combat missions the threat to the mission is the adversarial force), threat analysis includes identification and description of how each relevant characteristic of the operational area could hamper friendly mission accomplishment. The commander uses this information along with the descriptions of the relevant features of the operational area to shape the environment and choose the appropriate course of action for successful completion of his unit's mission.

IPB is an ongoing cyclical process composed of four steps. The first three steps are designed to compile information about specific features of the operational area. The fourth step consolidates this information to help predict enemy courses of action (COAs).

The four steps of the IPB process as described in current doctrine are

1. Define the battlefield area

2. Describe the battlefield's effects

3. Evaluate the threat

4. Develop enemy courses of action

The questions asked and answered by each of the four steps help to coordinate reconnaissance and surveillance (R&S); manage intelligence-collection efforts; supply location and asset information for the targeting process; and integrate battle damage assessment (BDA) into the execution of follow-on missions. Once the operation has begun, continuing the IPB process is essential for further situation development and COA assessment.

Each of the steps of the existing IPB process is discussed in more detail in this chapter. Later chapters of this report discuss how existing IPB doctrine might be modified to accommodate operations in urbanized terrain.

CURRENT DOCTRINAL IPB STEP ONE: DEFINE THE BATTLEFIELD AREA

IPB step one provides focus for the remaining steps of the process. Doctrinally, the intent of step one, *define the battlefield area*, is to

> focus the IPB effort on the areas and characteristics of the battlefield which will influence the command's mission and to acquire the intelligence needed to complete the IPB process in the degree of detail required to support the military decisionmaking process.[1]

---

[1]FM 34-130/MCRP 2-12A, *Intelligence Preparation of the Battlefield (Initial Draft)*, Washington, D.C.: Department of the Army, 1999, p. 2-1.

This includes

> identifying for further analysis specific features of the environment
> or activities within it, and the physical space where they exist, that
> may influence available [friendly and enemy] COAs or the com-
> mander's decisions.[2]

There are four tasks typically conducted as step one of IPB:

1. Define the area of operations

2. Define the area of interest

3. Define the battlespace

4. Gather available intelligence and identify intelligence gaps

The *area of operations* (AO) is

> a geographical area, including the airspace above, usually defined by
> lateral, forward and rear boundaries, assigned to a commander . . . in
> which he has responsibility and the authority to conduct military
> operations.[3]

Higher headquarters bases the size of the AO on mission, enemy, terrain, troops, time available, and civilian considerations (METT-TC)
as well as the tactics, techniques, and procedures (TTP) employed by
the unit.[4] Because the AO is the area in which most of the unit's assets will be deployed, much of the intelligence effort is focused on
this area.

The *area of interest* (AOI) is doctrinally defined as "the geographical
area from which information and intelligence are required to permit
planning or successful conduct of the command's operation. . . . The
limits of the AOI include each of the characteristics of the battlefield

---

[2]Ibid.

[3]FM 101-5-1/MCRP 5-2A, *Operational Terms and Graphics*, Washington, D.C.:
Department of the Army and U.S. Marine Corps, September 30, 1997, p. 1-10.

[4]The use of METT-TC rather than METT-T is based on drafts of emerging doctrine,
particularly Joint Publication 3-0, *Doctrine for Joint Operations*, and other Army and
Marine Corps manuals in which the role and effects associated with the presence of
civilians on the battlefield are deemed to warrant greater consideration.

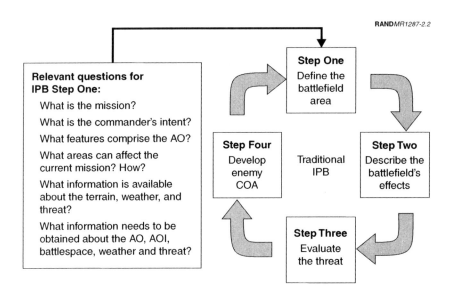

Figure 2.2—Doctrinal IPB Step One

environment identified as exerting an influence on available COAs or command decisions."[5] The delineation of the AOI is intended to help the command staff predict the elements beyond the AO that might influence the mission within it. As described in FM 34-130, the AOI is traditionally drawn as an area circumscribing the AO. This practice is based on Cold War practices that delineated the AOI based on the known effective ranges of the adversary's weapon systems. Such a practice is no longer practical.

As identified in Field Manual 34-7, *IEW for Stability Operations and Support Operations* (Initial Draft, November 1999), the elements that can affect the AO are not necessarily only those that are lethal to the friendly unit. The AOI should also incorporate any asset held by a combatant or noncombatant that could influence the friendly operation. FM 34-7, as well as Joint Publication (JP) 2-01.3, *Joint Tactics, Techniques and Procedures for Joint Intelligence Preparation of*

---

[5]FM 34-130/MCRP 2-12A, *Intelligence Preparation of the Battlefield (Coordinating Draft)*, Washington, D.C.: Department of the Army, 1999.

the Battlespace, illustrate the need to include such nontraditional elements as the location of an enemy accomplice supplying money and logistical support, refugee populations outside the AO dependent on water supplies within the AO, and international audiences susceptible to media reports originating from the AO. The inclusion of these noncombat elements suggests that the AOI might include areas not contiguous with the AO. It is important to note that the systems used to influence the AOI and battlespace are not limited to weaponry. Civil affairs (CA), public affairs (PA), psychological operations (PSYOP), and other assets have the capability to influence activity beyond the AO. Their effects should also be considered.

The *battlespace* is also identified as part of step one. Doctrinally, the battlespace is

> the conceptual physical volume in which the commander seeks to dominate the enemy. It expands and contracts in relation to the commander's ability to acquire and engage the enemy or can change as the commander's vision of the battlefield changes. It encompasses three dimensions and is influenced by the operational dimensions of time, tempo, depth and synchronization. It is not assigned by a higher commander nor is it constrained by assigned boundaries.[6]

Because the definition of the battlespace is based on the capabilities of the friendly unit to affect activities outside of the assigned AO, it might be significantly different from the AOI. For instance, the 1992 NEO (noncombatant evacuation operation) at the U.S. Embassy in Sierra Leone required soldiers to pick up U.S. nationals from their homes. The AOI in this case could have been those areas along the planned extraction routes where resistance was anticipated. The battlespace, however, might not have included these enclaves but could have included a police station friendly to the United States that could be called upon to quell a disturbance.

While determining the limits of the AO, AOI, and battlespace, the S2/G2/J2 begins to collect data on the relevant aspects of his area of responsibility (AOR), which consists of the AO, AOI, and the battlespace combined. This material includes such items as maps, geo-

---

[6]FM 101-5-1/MCRP 5-2A, *Operational Terms and Graphics,* p. 1-18.

The Democratic National Convention
Los Angeles, California
August 2000

During the 2000 Democratic National Convention, the Los Angeles County Sheriff's Department (LASD) was responsible for the safe transport of convention delegates between the Staples Center, located downtown, and over 240 hotels throughout the Southland. The AO for the LASD included a perimeter around the Staples Center itself, all of Los Angeles's major freeways, the side streets used to get to the hotels and the hotels themselves. Understanding the components of this AO required more than just knowing the physical topography of the roadways. It also required an understanding of the traffic conditions, street light operations, road conditions, locations of protestors, and possible alternate routes. Understanding the AO, and planning a mission that ensured success, required coordination with several different law enforcement agencies, each tasked to complete different activities, often in their own overlapping AOs. For instance, sniper positions along the major roadways were to be identified by the LASD but were controlled by other law enforcement agencies.

SOURCE: Notes for the 2000 Democratic National Convention held in Los Angeles, California; provided by Robert Galarneu, interviewed by the author on July 21, 2000.

Figure 2.3—Designating the Urban AO

logical surveys, demographic information, threat order of battle (OB), personality profiles, and historical accounts of activities in the area. By collecting and reviewing these products, the analyst is able to identify critical information gaps and begin to work with the commander to develop a list of relevant questions, referred to as the commander's critical information requirements (CCIR), that will drive intelligence collection for the operation.

CURRENT DOCTRINAL IPB STEP TWO: DESCRIBE THE BATTLEFIELD'S EFFECTS

Doctrinally, the second step of the IPB process, *describe the battlefield's effects*, requires the analyst to demonstrate how the weather, terrain, and other characteristics of the battlefield can affect both friendly and enemy operations within a given AO, AOI, and battlespace. The stated intent of this step is to allow the commander to quickly choose and exploit the terrain (and associated weather, politics, economics or other relevant factors) that best supports the friendly mission.[7]

For the friendly force to be best able to exploit the terrain, IPB step two involves two tasks. The first is to identify the military aspects of the operational area: What exists in the area that can influence a mission? The second task describes how the identified features will affect a unit's operation in the area.

Distinguishing the military aspects of the terrain generally entails identifying how the relief, structural, and vegetation features of the area serve or interfere with a military purpose. These military purposes are categorized in what are commonly referred to as OCOKA factors: observation and fields of fire, concealment and cover, obstacles, key terrain, and avenues of approach. Each terrain feature is scrutinized to determine how it might be included in each of these categories. Once the military aspects of the terrain are identified, they are used to describe how military operations are affected. For instance, descriptions of how the obstacles along a certain avenue of approach will affect maneuver formations, or how trees providing concealment can be used to hide part of all of a unit, are generally provided.

Military aspects of weather include fog, heat, rain, and snow. These conditions can directly affect operations by degrading the capabilities of some equipment (e.g., the cameras of aerial vehicles may be unable to see through fog, soldiers require special equipment for the snow). These conditions can be exploited by either side to provide tactical or strategic advantage. For instance, fog conditions can be used to mask troop movement. Weather analysis is also relevant for its effect on the noncombatant population. Rain can create sewage overflow problems in refugee camps, a condition that may have to be managed by the friendly force in order to avoid disease and panic.

What elements comprise the "other" conditions that need to be evaluated as part of IPB step two is mission dependent, but they could encompass such factors as population demographics, rules of

---

[7]FM 34-130/MCRP 2-12A, *Intelligence Preparation of the Battlefield (Initial Draft)*, Washington, D.C.: Department of the Army, 1999, p. 2-1.

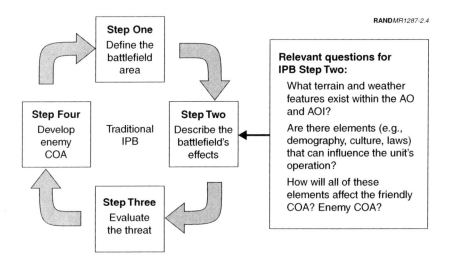

RAND*MR1287-2.4*

Figure 2.4—Doctrinal IPB Step Two

engagement, and the regulations imposed by international treaties. These military factors can have significant effects on the operation. Each must be scrutinized for its immediate and derivative effects on the operation. For instance, rules of engagement have notoriously influenced U.S. ability to operate on a level playing field with a relatively unscrupulous adversary. For example, soldiers should know how to handle a situation in which an adversary has positioned himself behind civilian shields, as was the case in Mogadishu, before he or she confronts the problem in combat.

The demographic components of the "other" conditions should also be more than a listing of statistical information about the population. Intelligence on how the living conditions have changed as a result of the operation and how members of the population are dealing with these changes are examples of the kind of intelligence that can be derived from demographic information. This intelligence can then be used to better predict how the demographic conditions can affect military operations.

Overall, step two helps paint the picture of what conditions the unit could face and helps the intelligence analyst identify areas and times of potential operational superiority that the friendly force might exploit.

CURRENT DOCTRINAL IPB STEP THREE: EVALUATE THE THREAT

Step three of IPB, *evaluate the threat,* develops a profile of the enemy. The purpose of this step is to

> develop threat models which accurately portray how the adversary doctrinally operates under normal conditions.[8]

The analyst seeks to determine enemy composition, strength, disposition, tactics, goals, and vulnerabilities by using information provided by national intelligence agencies and the unit's organic intelligence assets.

FM 34-130/MCRP 2-12A, *Intelligence Preparation of the Battlefield,* clearly defines the process by which the intelligence analyst should develop a model of a conventional enemy. For example, intelligence staffs are required to identify threat force structure, weapons inventories, key leaders, doctrinal formations, and TTP. Using historical information on how the known enemy generally employs his tactics, intelligence analysts are then able to create templates that portray how the enemy might operate in the area of operations.

FM 34-7 (Initial Draft), *IEW for Stability Operations and Support Operations,* supplements this traditional analysis with an investigation of all elements that might hinder mission accomplishment. Incorporating terrain, population, man-made objects, and the psychology of both threat and friendly forces, the analyst seeks to uncover all aspects of the environment that pose a threat to successful completion of the mission. This manual highlights the fact that threats are mission dependent and therefore not consistent for every type of operation. For instance, a "threat" in a humanitarian operation might be an inadequate water supply, while a threat in a combat operation could be a determined, well-equipped, and organized force. Regardless of threat, the evaluation must include a thorough

---

[8]Ibid., p. 3-1.

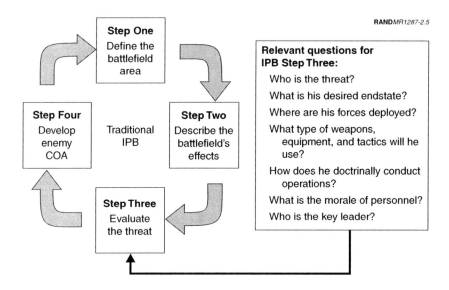

Figure 2.5—Doctrinal IPB Step Three

investigation of how it can directly and indirectly affect the friendly unit and its success in accomplishing the assigned mission.

CURRENT DOCTRINAL IPB STEP FOUR: DEVELOP ENEMY COURSES OF ACTION

Step four of IPB, *develop enemy courses of action*, incorporates the first three steps of the process into a picture of how the enemy will use terrain, weather, and its existing assets to achieve its goals within the designated AO, AOI, and battlespace. FM 34-130/MCRP 2-12A defines this step as "the identification and development of the threat plans adopted by them to accomplish their mission, thus showing their direct impact on the accomplishment of the friendly mission or stated goals."[9] The resulting products are templates depicting predicted enemy behavior throughout the AO. A consolidated list of all potential adversary COAs should be developed during this step. At a

_____

[9]Ibid., p. 1-7.

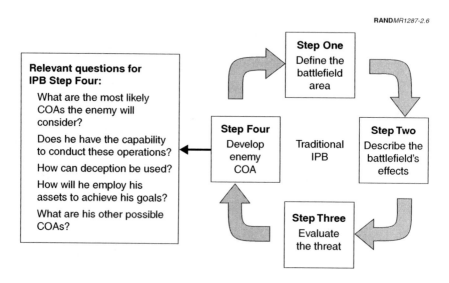

RAND*MR1287-2.6*

Relevant questions for IPB Step Four:

What are the most likely COAs the enemy will consider?

Does he have the capability to conduct these operations?

How can deception be used?

How will he employ his assets to achieve his goals?

What are his other possible COAs?

Step One
Define the battlefield area

Step Four
Develop enemy COA

Traditional IPB

Step Two
Describe the battlefield's effects

Step Three
Evaluate the threat

Figure 2.6—Doctrinal IPB Step Four

minimum, the list will include "all COAs the adversary's doctrine considers appropriate to the current situation and accomplishment of his likely objectives [and] all adversary COAs which could significantly influence the friendly mission, even if the adversary doctrine considers them suboptimal under current conditions, and all adversary COAs indicated by recent activities or events."[10]

Named areas of interest (NAIs) are associated with each templated enemy COA. NAI are designated points that will help confirm or deny a particular enemy COA. The formal definition is "a point or area along a particular avenue of approach through which enemy activity is expected to occur. Activity or lack of activity within an NAI will help to confirm or deny a particular enemy course of action."[11] For instance, many maneuver NAI are key intersections along designated avenues of approach. By placing intelligence-gathering assets at these locations, the COA chosen by the adversary can be deter-

---

[10]JP 2-01.3, *Joint Intelligence Preparation of the Battlespace,* Washington, D.C.: United States Joint Chiefs of Staff, 2000, p. II-57.

[11]FM 101-5-1/MCRP 5-2A, *Operational Terms and Graphics,* p. 1-107.

mined based on whether his force goes left, right, or in another direction.

Also included as part of the overall enemy COA development is the identification of high-payoff targets (HPT) and high-value targets (HVT). HPT are targets the loss of which by the threat "will contribute to the success of the friendly force course of action."[12] HVT are "assets that the threat commander requires for the successful completion of a specific course of action."[13] Targeting these assets is therefore critical to the successful accomplishment of the friendly mission. Identification of HVT may also lead to elucidation of the enemy's center of gravity (COG), which is doctrinally defined as "the hub of all power and movement, on which everything depends."[14]

IDENTIFICATION AND INCORPORATION OF INTELLIGENCE REQUIREMENTS: HOW IPB FOCUSES OPERATIONAL PLANNING AND INTELLIGENCE GATHERING

IPB provides an effective framework for identifying missing information and incorporating new information into the existing intelligence picture. Because each step of IPB seeks to answer a category of questions regarding the context in which the unit is deployed, an unanswered query clearly highlights what information is missing and whether this omission is relevant to the operation. Salient questions are then prioritized as intelligence requirements (IR) and are included in an overall intelligence-collection plan. The most critical intelligence requirements, known as the commander's critical information requirements (CCIR), are categorized based on the type of information necessary to fulfill them. CCIR include three categories:

---

[12]Ibid., p. 1-83.
[13]Ibid.
[14]Ibid., p. 1-18.

1. **Priority intelligence requirements (PIR).** Those intelligence requirements for which a commander has an anticipated and stated priority in his task of planning and decisionmaking.[15]

2. **Essential elements of friendly information (EEFI).** Key questions likely to be asked by adversary officials and intelligence systems about specific friendly intentions, capabilities, and activities so they can obtain answers critical to their operational effectiveness.[16]

3. **Friendly force information requirements (FFIR).** Information the commander and staff need about the forces available for the operation. This includes personnel, maintenance, supply, ammunition, and leadership capabilities.[17]

The IPB framework also has an additional benefit: Its structure allows analysts to incorporate what might initially appear to be extraneous information. Because each of the steps of IPB seeks to identify relevant information about a particular aspect of the operational area, any information that is obtained can be slotted into the appropriate step.

Overall, IPB is a framework to help structure thought, compose appropriate questions, and incorporate information when it becomes available. It is the flexible nature of IPB that allows it to adapt to a multitude of different contingencies on a myriad of different terrain types during a variety of operations. IPB is most useful when it is constantly being reevaluated in terms of the mission the unit must accomplish. How IPB can be used to successfully complete an urban mission is the subject of subsequent chapters.

---

[15]Ibid., p. 1-124.

[16]Ibid., p. 1-62.

[17]Ibid., p. 1-72.

Chapter Three
CHALLENGES POSED BY URBANIZED TERRAIN

When tasked with urban operations, most soldiers think of buildings.

Ralph Peters
"The Human Terrain of Urban Operations"

There is more to urban areas that at first glance seems to define them. There are "[h]undreds, more likely thousands, tens of thousands, or even millions of buildings, vehicles, people, acreage, rooms, windows, streets, underground passageways, and much else [that] make up the totality."[1] The densities of both people and buildings in urban areas create familiar operational difficulties for a deployed force. Structures and public works infrastructure inhibit maneuver and firepower, open and close fields of fire, and severely degrade command and control (C2) capabilities.[2] Urban residents create conditions for restrictive rules of engagement, increase stress on soldiers and logistics capabilities, and confuse threat identification. The nature of built-up areas themselves changes over time. The effects of rubble, population movements, and psychological strain on soldiers operating within an area dense with information and decision points degrade situational awareness and affect morale and decisionmaking capabilities.

---

[1]Russell W. Glenn, *Heavy Matter: Urban Operations' Density of Challenges,* Santa Monica, CA: RAND, MR-1239-JS/A, 2000, p. 2.

[2]The effects of multidimensional warfare on command and control are addressed in Sean J.A. Edwards, *Freeing Mercury's Wings: Improving Tactical Communications in Cities,* Santa Monica, CA: RAND, MR-1316-A, 2001.

It is obvious that the densities of urban areas present more than operational challenges. The same factors that complicate the operational aspects of MOUT—the underlying terrain, buildings, infrastructure, and people—also stress the existing methods of intelligence analysis and decisionmaking at all levels of war. IPB is one such casualty of urban operations. Although IPB methodology is sound—the series of steps used to evaluate extant operational conditions—traditional IPB doctrine, as discussed in the previous chapter, is still based mainly on Cold War ideas that assume most engagements are combat operations against a single, known enemy on open terrain. IPB doctrine, therefore, is written based on those assumptions, none of which remains true. Additionally, unique urban attributes provide large quantities of information that are not readily incorporated into existing IPB techniques. For IPB to remain effective for urban operations, its analysis must include a city's unique attributes—buildings, infrastructure, and people—along with an evaluation of the attributes traditionally included in IPB, namely, the underlying terrain and the known threat. Each of these significant features of a city, and the dilemmas each poses for a unit's operational and intelligence functions, are the subject of this chapter.

UNDERLYING TERRAIN

Soldiers, particularly those in intelligence staff positions, are accustomed to analyzing the relief features of open terrain. Analysis of this type generally includes such tasks as identification of high ground, categorization of mobility corridors, and designation of key terrain. Maps of an area of open terrain, often of no greater resolution than 1:50,000, are usually descriptive enough to make tactical and operational choices about maneuver and the use of firepower. Areas of restricted terrain and severely restricted terrain are identified on the map based on slope, ground cover, numbers and types of obstacles, and the availability of concealment and cover.

The topographical factors that are considered standard elements of analysis for traditional, nonurban operations are often thought much less important for analyzing urbanized terrain. But the natural terrain features that lie beneath urban edifices do, in fact, significantly influence unit operations. They dictate where buildings can be constructed and how streets align, thereby influencing a unit's scheme of maneuver. In addition, the slope of roads within urban areas often follows the underlying terrain's natural contours. These examples suggest that the terrain features within an urban area remain critical to unit operations and thus must be included in the overall terrain analysis of a city.

MCWP 3-35.3, *Military Operations on Urbanized Terrain,* and FM 34-130/MCRP2-12A, *Intelligence Preparation of the Battlefield (Coordinating Draft)*, particularly the new appendix "IPB for MOUT," address how to investigate the underlying terrain of a city. These publications describe how a city's layout affects a large unit's ability to penetrate or envelop it. They also explain how the underlying terrain affects a city's street patterns as well as its distance from other urban areas.

What these manuals do not include are discussions of how a city's history, ecology, economy, politics, or culture can be influenced by the ground on which it sits. For instance, the historical significance of many sites in Israel, such as Temple Mount, is often more salient to the essence of a conflict than are the buildings that mark them. Chicago is a megalopolis in large part because of its proximity to trade routes that provided the primary means of moving goods from East to West during the late 19th and early 20th centuries.[3]

BUILDINGS

Buildings complicate all aspects of military operations in urban areas. Their composition, frontages, size, and window locations affect force positioning and weapons deployment considerations. Angles, displacement, surface reflection, and antenna locations influence communications and intelligence collection. Considerations such as snipers, rubble, booby traps, interfloor movement, and the like are often directly related to urban construction. For instance, buildings increase the numbers of viable approaches for foot soldiers but limit them for other ground maneuver elements. Snipers, able to hide at any elevation, can become a highly potent weapon for any

---

[3]William Cronon, *Nature's Metropolis: Chicago and the Great West,* New York: W. W. Norton & Company, 1991.

size force. Rubble is often used for hide sites, booby trap locations, or obstacles. The psychological effects of urban operations are also augmented by buildings. Being able to maneuver and shoot at a multitude of angles and through walls, ceilings, and floors creates psychological and physiological stress in any force.

Buildings also create possible social, cultural, or political dilemmas. Places of worship, government edifices, schools, hospitals, parks, and the like all need to be understood in terms of their significance. Because many cities are peppered with culturally and politically significant buildings, analysts seeking to describe cities face the challenge of accurately identifying and describing them in order to avoid a political faux pas. Consider the bombing of the Chinese embassy in Belgrade during NATO air operations in 2000. Misguided targeting that allowed a bomb to drop on the wrong location severely strained relations between the United States and China and created considerable embarrassment for the U.S. intelligence community. This error could have been avoided had up-to-date information on key cultural and political locations been on hand.

Buildings can impede intelligence-collection efforts. The amount of information that must be collected and assessed regarding structures in urban areas is enormous. Ideally, information about a particular building should include its floor plan in addition to a description of its building materials. Who owns a particular building, who its tenants are, and how it is connected to water and power facilities might also be valuable information. Collecting all of this information, or even knowing which buildings to collect it for, might prove overwhelming. The challenge of assimilating it into an overall analysis of an urban operational area is equally staggering.

Buildings also conceal other relevant operational data. Interior mobility corridors cannot be identified. The condition of the interior can sometimes only be surmised; floor and ceiling stability, the possibility of exposed electrical wires or sewage pipes, and the amount of debris inside a building are indeterminable. The presence of people, both combatant and noncombatant, is consistently questionable. People could be hiding inside buildings, basements, or alleyways waiting to ambush a patrol or waiting for that same patrol to bring them food.

Understanding the risks buildings pose to friendly units operating in urban areas is critical to successful completion of any mission. Luckily, urban construction has received the bulk of attention in U.S. armed forces MOUT doctrinal materials. FM 34-130/MCWP 2-12A, *Intelligence Preparation of the Battlefield (Coordinating Draft)*, FM 5-33, *Terrain Analysis,* FM 90-10, *Military Operations on Urbanized Terrain,* and MCWP 3-35.3, *Military Operations on Urbanized Terrain,* establish procedures for investigating and analyzing construction's effects on the deployment of men, materiel, and weapons within an urban area. These manuals describe how to assess the layout of a city, how to analyze the structural characteristics of most buildings, how to deploy and maneuver the appropriate weapons based on these structural characteristics, and how to perform a variety of tactical actions such as clearing a room and breaching walls. In addition to these manuals, Ralph Ellefson's work, *Urban Terrain Zone Characteristics*, and FM 90-10-1, *An Infantryman's Guide to Urban Combat,* set clear guidelines for deciphering building type based on outward appearance. Overall, these resources do an adequate job of describing how to assess the city's construction characteristics and how urban layout affects maneuver. But they are written in a way that stresses the desire to operate around or pass through cities rather than operate within them.

Missing from doctrine are prescriptions for achieving situational awareness in urban areas, which might prove critical at the tactical level where street widths, odd building construction types or building mixes, incomprehensible street names, and the indescribable shantytown all may disorient the soldier mid-operation. No one versed in MOUT can forget the story of the U.S. Rangers separated from each other in life-threatening circumstances during the 1993 firefight in Mogadishu, Somalia. Soldiers became disoriented in no small part because of the lack of intelligence on the city's structural conditions, street widths, and lack of clear landmarks to navigate them.

Current doctrine also lacks discussion of how urban combatants can use a city's construction to support their tactics. Other than the small number of tactics described in FM 90-10-1, how the friendly or enemy force can use buildings to enhance their own tactics or degrade the opponent's performance is not discussed. Much can be gained from recent studies on the topic, however. The most well-studied urban tactical modifications resulting from the use of buildings are those of the Chechens and Russians in their recent campaigns. Tim Thomas addresses the effectiveness of Chechen small-unit tactics, including the use of rocket-propelled grenades (RPGs), booby traps, and swarming techniques.[4] Using these lessons learned to instruct intelligence analysts in the art of urban warfare may help the S2/G2/J2/C2 better assess the capabilities and limitations presented by a city's streets and buildings.

INFRASTRUCTURE

In urban areas, buildings and people are interconnected with phone lines, roadways, sidewalks, electrical wires, drainage pipes, and gas mains, the layout of which often cannot be easily surmised. These connections pose dilemmas for command and control, the health and welfare of a unit and the civilian population, logistics, and other aspects of an operation.

Public utilities, both their generation locations and supply infrastructure, can be significant obstacles to maneuver, communications, and the use of firepower. Broken water hydrants can deplete a municipality's water resources. Phone and electrical lines inhibit helicopter airspace.

The capability of utilities to affect many regions of the city gives them the potential to be used as weapons or as weapons platforms. For instance, if the water flow into a city can be controlled, a motivated individual can intentionally limit that flow and create an urgent need that the army must address. This manipulation of the water supply serves as a potentially lethal weapon (people can become dehydrated or overheated) as well as a weapon of information warfare (fear of having an adversary control a critical need). As a weapon's platform, this same water supply can be tainted with a biological agent that can infect anyone who drinks it, creating disease of epidemic proportions as well as considerable terror in the population.

---

[4]See Timothy L. Thomas, *Some Asymmetric Lessons of Urban Combat: The Battle of Grozny*, Fort Leavenworth, KS: Foreign Military Studies Office, 1999; and Timothy L. Thomas, *From Grozny to Belgrade: Constructing the "Mental Toolbox" of Asymmetric Urban Conflict Options*, Fort Leavenworth, KS: Foreign Military Studies Office, 1999.

RAND*MR1287-3.1*

PHOTO: Jamison Jo Medby.

Figure 3.1—Utility and Public Works Infrastructure (Tijuana, Mexico)

Government buildings, hospitals, religious centers, and schools are laden with legal and moral dilemmas that must be understood and resolved prior to operations. Typical U.S. ROE and laws of land warfare might protect religious centers from use or destruction. An adversary might not feel bound by these regulations and intentionally target a building. Understanding how an adversary might abide by similar conventions or exploit them is critical to keeping the upper hand.

Current doctrine only peripherally addresses the moral and legal issues surrounding the use of public utilities and culturally significant infrastructure in military operations. FM 34-130 mentions only the legal restrictions associated with protected buildings. The Marine Corps *Urban Generic Information Requirements Handbook (GIRH)* does an excellent job of addressing the complications created by public works and public infrastructure. The *Urban GIRH* includes a section devoted to questions about the location, composition, and materials associated with public works. The handbook also lists questions about the significance of infrastructure like utilities and religious centers. Together, these doctrinal materials begin to assist the intelligence analyst in deciphering the key aspects of urban infrastructure that can affect operations.

PEOPLE

The aforementioned assets of an urban landscape are largely inanimate and lack cognition. Given enough time and resources, they can be identified, catalogued, and analyzed despite their number and density. More challenging to analyze are the people who exist within an urban area. As the only thinking component of an operational area, people have the capacity to significantly modify operations. There are several reasons why urban populations threaten operations and their attendant intelligence support functions. The hypotheses regarding the kinds of dilemmas posed by urban populations, which we shall use throughout this report, are summarized in Table 3.1.

What is stressed throughout the remainder of the text is that urban populations are extremely heterogeneous. The overall population is composed of several groups, each with its own interests. Relationships between groups might be congenial, hostile, or dependent.

Understanding this diversity and complexity requires a significant amount of mental effort and flexibility.

The cultural tendencies of urban residents might be very different from what American soldiers are accustomed to. Food, habits, living conditions, laws, religious customs, and beliefs may initially distance a soldier from the city's residents. The differences must be appreciated by the friendly force in order to achieve and maintain legitimacy within a foreign operational area.

Cultural differences can also affect tactical efforts. In Mogadishu, for instance, groups of civilians protected Somali gunmen by using their own bodies as cover. This unfamiliar tactic created a dilemma for soldiers constrained by the rules of engagement and the laws of land warfare. Perhaps if the practice of using unarmed combatants as shields had been known before the mission began, a clearer response could have been dictated to the soldiers who were deployed.

Table 3.1

Urban Populations' Effects on Operations and Analysis

1. Urban populations are composed of many groups and subgroups.
2. Each group has its own needs, interests, intentions, and capabilities
3. Relationships that exist among groups might play critical roles in operations.
4. Cultural differences can strain relations between the friendly force and the resident population if not understood and appreciated.
5. People going about their daily routines can unwittingly hamper friendly objectives.
6. The resident population has survival and living needs that cannot be ignored.
7. Urban population groups and subgroups increase the number of elements to be identified and assessed as potential threats to the friendly force. They also increase the number of potential groups able to assist the friendly force.
8. The presence of noncombatants can escalate tactical actions to episodes of strategic importance.
9. Current doctrine often engenders an "us-versus-them" mentality that might create gaps in intelligence and barriers to complete analysis.

People can unwittingly disrupt army tactical activities simply by going about their daily routines. People can get in the way of a deployed force, creating obstacles to maneuver. They may also provide concealment for an adversary seeking to move closer to the friendly force. Chechen insurgents routinely wore civilian clothes in their efforts to blend in with the local civilian populace and avoid detection by Russian military personnel.

Support of noncombatants can divert resources from mission-related activities. For instance, a combat operation that displaces a significant number of residents, or disrupts critical public works functions, might necessitate redirecting unit resources away from their originally intended recipients, as it did when Allied Forces liberated Paris in 1944. During that operation, fuel supplies and supply aircraft scheduled to be used for an Air Transport Command training exercise had to be diverted in order to haul necessary commodities to the city.[5] Understanding that the possibilities exist for these types of occurrences can help a unit determine its capabilities to respond.

The abundant population groups and subgroups inherent to cities make threat identification difficult. Unlike more traditional operations on open terrain, where merely spotting an unknown entity would assist in deciphering friend from foe, urban areas are packed with individuals and groups that might have the capabilities, interests, or intentions that can threaten a unit's mission. An analyst will not be able to distinguish urban friend from foe just by looking at him. During the World Trade Organization meeting in Seattle during 1999, several groups gathered near the meeting site to protest. Many of the groups were peaceful, using only words to make their case and following the legal guidelines for assembly. Other groups, some protesting and others acting as opportunists, vandalized property and caused injury to themselves and others. All these groups often commingled in the same location. Additionally, members of the peaceful groups were co-opted by more militant ones and assisted in forming human chains to shield violent protestors. All of this left law enforcement officials with the difficult task of identifying the true troublemakers. Knowing what groups exist within the operational

---

[5]Forrest C. Pogue, *United States Army in World War II: European Theater of Operations, the Supreme Command,* Washington D.C.: Department of the Army, 1954, pp. 258–259.

area and understanding the interests and intentions of each can help military staffs plan operations—complete with public affairs (PA), civil affairs (CA) and psychological operations (PSYOP) plans to help ensure that the less adversarial groups remain more closely aligned with friendly force objectives.

When faced with a situation similar to the WTO example, it is easy to see how any participant can adopt a mentality that splits the actors involved into only two camps: those "with us" and those "against us." It is important for the intelligence analyst to recognize, however, that not all sectors of the population, including those that at first glance may appear threatening, necessarily work against the friendly force. Individuals and groups of all backgrounds can be co-opted or influenced by the friendly force to serve a friendly or benign objective. For instance, during World War II the U.S. Navy worked covertly with the Mafia in New York City in order to secure the New York harbor from German U-boats believed to be torpedoing ships there. The Mafia, whose members had strong patriotic leanings, also had "a stranglehold on all dock activities in the port of New York and . . . [was] in a sound position to monitor any subversive activity along the waterfront."[6] This capability provided needed intelligence to the Navy for its counterespionage and security tasks. New York authorities therefore agreed to permit a Navy-Mafia alliance to operate at the port for the "greater good of national security."[7] Clearly, the Mafia was probably not the Navy's preferred choice of ally, given its status as an adversary to law enforcement (and the military by extension). But because the Mafia had the capability to protect U.S. ships and the interest to help in the war effort, the temporary alliance worked.

People present in a city also raise the stakes of tactical operations. Potentially, the impact of any event can be raised to the strategic level of war. The "strategic corporal" may be interviewed or filmed by media in the area.[8] Collateral damage or civilian casualties are

---

[6]Carlo D'este, *Bitter Victory: The Battle for Sicily 1943*, Glasgow: William Collins Sons and Co. Ltd, 1988, p. 625.

[7]Ibid.

[8]The concept of the strategic corporal relates to the capability of any tactically deployed soldier, marine, or airman to affect an operation at the strategic level of war due to the presence of media.

often fodder for sensationalized news that can enrage both local and international audiences.

Obviously, the dilemmas posed by urban operations are many. Being able to address them can only be done with significant effort and a new approach to operations and analysis.

SHORTFALLS IN CURRENT IPB DOCTRINE

As discussed in the previous chapter, IPB is a method that helps determine the best friendly force course of action and seeks to demonstrate how the terrain, weather, and threat conditions within an assigned area can affect friendly operations. IPB does this by providing a framework for organizing data and highlighting intelligence gaps. As a methodology for organizing and assessing data, IPB is sound. Current IPB doctrine, however, is based on Cold War mindsets that assume most engagements the Army will encounter are combat operations unfolding against a known enemy on open terrain. Urban characteristics do not easily fit into this Cold War paradigm for two main reasons:

1. Current doctrine minimizes the salient elements of urban operations—underlying terrain, buildings, infrastructure, and people—by considering them mostly as "other" factors that can affect unit operations.

2. Because these elements are minimized, current doctrine does not effectively incorporate their potential effects on the operation into the command estimate process. "Other" elements are traditionally analyzed only as a "battlefield effect." They are not usually integrated during threat identification, threat analysis, or area of interest identification, for instance.

The first dilemma is one of identification of features salient to the unfolding operation. The second is an issue pertaining to the process of intelligence analysis.

Identification of unique urban characteristics is being incorporated into new doctrinal publications. Most recent doctrinal adjustments to accommodate IPB for MOUT contain much relevant information on underlying terrain and building feature identification. This construction-centric approach, however, minimizes consideration of a city's populations and rarely mentions the interactive nature of urban infrastructure. There are some promising exceptions. FM 34-7, *IEW for Stability Operations and Support Operations,* begins to address the need to incorporate the population as a key component for defining and understanding the operational area. The Marine Corps *Urban GIRH* similarly includes population considerations as one of the key components to be analyzed as part of any operation.

Discussion of how the IPB process can be adjusted to assimilate all of the extraordinary information created by force deployments to urban areas is rare in current doctrine. It is apparently assumed that urban characteristics, like those of the jungle or desert, are most conveniently analyzed merely as conditions of the battlefield that should be included only in step two, *describe the battlefield's effects.* Little effort is given to depicting how these extant conditions can also be included in the other three steps of IPB.

The chapters that follow contain suggestions for improving the current IPB process to ensure it remains effective given the vast amounts of information it must include for any type of urban operation. The names of the steps are slightly modified (see Figure 3.2) in order to ensure that the IPB process is not constrained by the mindsets described above, and to better reflect each step's function. These modifications aim to expand thinking beyond combat operations and seek to incorporate the suggested ideas proposed throughout the rest of this text.

The Four Steps of IPB	
Traditional Label	**Suggested Label**
1. Define the battlefield area	1. Define the operating environment
2. Describe the battlefield's effects	2. Describe the operating environment's effects
3. Evaluate the threat	3. Identify and evaluate threats and relevant influences
4. Develop enemy courses of action	4. Develop non-U.S. courses of action

Figure 3.2—Suggested Labels for the Four Steps of IPB

Chapter Four

IPB FOR URBAN OPERATIONS STEP ONE: DEFINE THE OPERATING ENVIRONMENT

Every city is unique. Some are robust and resilient, while others are fragile and unable to cope with daily demands, let alone military actions. Some cities, particularly in the developing world, can barely provide basic water, sewage, power, transport, garbage collection, and public health services. Military actions in some cities, such as Hong Kong, New York, Frankfurt, Seoul and Singapore, would endanger the very economic stability of the nation—and the planet. Military actions in other cities may have only local consequences.

> Lester Grau and Jacob Kipp
> "Urban Combat: Confronting the Specter"

Military commanders at any level must have sufficient control to allow coordination of the many actions undertaken by subordinate units; they must be able to modify plans rapidly and effectively so as to retain the initiative. That is difficult during any high-tempo operation; it is an even greater challenge when the density of high-tempo operations is such that it can overwhelm traditional decisionmaking processes and other command and control procedures.

> Russell W. Glenn
> *Heavy Matter: Urban Operations' Density of Challenges*

Step one of traditional IPB, *define the battlefield area,* is intended to define the areas of greatest concern as a commander conducts his mission. Recall that this step requires the delineation of the area of operations (which is typically defined by higher headquarters), area of interest, and battlespace. As these areas are circumscribed, information that can be used to describe them is collected, and missing information is requested and prioritized as intelligence requirements

(IR). In operations conducted on open terrain, the delineated areas are typically configured to suit the maneuver, command and control, and logistics components of the unit. As a result, the areas are decidedly two-dimensional in the sense that most of the emphasis is on the firepower and maneuver capabilities of friend and foe. The area of interest is generally drawn in cognizance of the enemy's doctrinal capabilities to project power into this AO. The AO and battlespace are defined based on the known capabilities of friendly units.

Relying on a two-dimensional, Red versus Blue approach to defining the commander's areas of concern does not adequately describe the volume and density of activity that occurs in built-up areas. For instance, the 1942 battle for Stalingrad, like many others in the past century, was frequently a building-to-building, room-to-room fight in which the "frontline" between opposing units was no more than a hallway or city street. Ranges were such that the toss of a grenade or "snap firing" of a rifle were the appropriate actions for those who sought to survive. An attack could come from any direction: right, left; forward, rearward; above, below. Urban combat, with very short ranges, denser and smaller engagement areas, and different weapons selection might dictate that a unit's area of operation be delineated as a single building or even a specific floor. Today's doctrine provides little guidance for how this should be done.

Urban operations mandate reconsideration of current procedures for AO and AOI designation decisions for other reasons as well. The plethora of information about a city and its inhabitants can overwhelm units deployed in a modern built-up area. Urban environments deluge collectors with so much information that guidance on how to decide what to report is essential. Such selection inherently means that the individuals performing reconnaissance must interpret what they see, hear, or otherwise sense. Age-old truths such as having reconnaissance elements report what they observe without interpretation may now be infeasible. Doctrine and training must both account for such fundamental changes.

As discussed in Chapter Two, the intent of the first step in IPB, *define the battlefield area*, is to identify for further analysis specific features of the environment or activities within it, and the physical space where they exist, that may influence available COAs or the commander's decisions.[1]

The three main objectives of this step are to

• Delineate the areas that will affect a unit's operation.

• Identify significant characteristics of the environment.

• Identify gaps in knowledge about these characteristics.

The first objective requires specification of an organization's area of operations, area of interest, and battlespace. Significant characteristics are anything that will affect a commander's decisions or a unit's operations. The shortfall between the relevant information on hand and the information needed to successfully execute an assigned mission comprises the intelligence gap that should be closed before the operation begins, if at all possible. Proposed in the remainder of this chapter are tools that can be used to fulfill these objectives. The ideas presented herein are again intended to suggest new and/or different ways of approaching urban dilemmas. They can be used independently or together, in any type of urban operation, depending on the needs of the commander and his staff.

DEFINING THE URBAN AREA OF OPERATIONS

The procedures for delineating an urban area of operations (AO) are fundamentally little different from those used for other terrain. The same tools—METT-TC, TTP, and the desired end state—facilitate the analysis, though the elements considered in each may be both more numerous and more complex.

METT-TC analysis in support of urban operations is often more complicated than when the *mission* involves a readily identified enemy on open terrain. Specified and implied tasks may be very heterogeneous and will often include such diverse responsibilities as combat actions directed against the enemy, support activities to

_____
[1]FM 34-130/MCRP 5-2A, *Intelligence Preparation of the Battlefield*, Washington, D.C.: Department of the Army, 1994, p. 2-2.

ensure that civilians do not needlessly suffer, and stability requirements only marginally related to the maneuver and combat support
demands. The result may be less-straightforward mission state-
ments or missions accompanied by a far greater number of specified
and implied tasks. Picking out the essential tasks from this mass
becomes especially difficult. In addition, actions taken by a friendly
or opposing unit can lead to several unintended consequences. The
1968 fighting in Hue, for instance, caused large numbers of South
Vietnamese civilians to seek refuge with their American allies, placing unanticipated demands on U.S. logistics and tactical units. The
Marine Corps has articulated such possibilities in its "three-block
war" concept: three adjacent city blocks may simultaneously present
a commander with combat, stability, and support taskings. Mission
articulation needs to balance these myriad demands with unit
capabilities when defining areas of operation.

Each of the other attributes of METT-TC may be similarly complicated during urban operations. The *enemy* can include a recogniz-
ably uniformed adversary, but threat considerations will also have to
review many noncombatant, police, and paramilitary groups. Some
of these will favor the enemy, others friendly forces, while yet others
will seek only to be left alone by opposing factions. Even this too-
simply states the probable state of affairs. Groups are fickle in their
favoritism. Their dispositions may repeatedly change in response to
propaganda, coercion, or other pressures. Further, demographic
groups are by no means homogeneous in their support; a clan
aligned with one side may well have members with agendas diverg-
ing from those of their leaders.

Terrain includes not only the natural surface confronted during any
military undertaking, but also the aforementioned structures on it,
beneath it, and the infrastructure throughout. Building construction
type will influence the number of soldiers needed for a particular
mission and the type of equipment they will require. Yet analysis
must delve far deeper than simple identification of a feature's characteristics. The number of such features per unit space (density) and
the density of features within features (e.g., rooms within apartments
within an apartment building) will similarly have a significant influence on the quantity and composition of a force selected for a given

urban mission.[2] In addition, there might exist a single street, avenue, or boulevard that might be assigned as its own AO because of buildings of religious, governmental, or cultural importance; such as LeLoi Street in Hue or Pennsylvania Avenue in Washington, D.C.

The *troops available* for actions in built-up areas cannot be figured using traditional force design; the number of tasks and varied terrain may demand extraordinary force ratios, nontraditional force structures, or other adjustments. The *time* necessary for an urban operation cannot be extrapolated from that needed to maneuver on less-complex terrain. The urban topography increases the overall surface area that the proposed mission will involve; intersections and multiple layers of "ground" increase the number of fronts that drain a unit of men, materiel, and time. Finally, *civilians* complicate matters not only from the perspective of threat as noted above, but also from that of the support they require to survive, the constraints their presence imposes on friendly force firepower employment, and the need to coordinate with agencies seeking to assist those in need. The density of noncombatants will impact on the tactics, techniques, and procedures most appropriate for a mission, as it will on the demand for food, water, medical care, and the likelihood of epidemics. Whereas rural environments generally contain fairly homogeneous social groups, the requirements for cultural awareness in towns and cities are complicated by the multiplicity of indigenous and international demographic factions. In short, buildings, infrastructure, and diverse populations tend to introduce intricacies into every element of the process of defining the area of operations.

Compared to other types of operations, civilian considerations have a disproportionately large influence on urban operations. Social and

---

[2]For more information on how density of all types affects urban operations, see Russell W. Glenn, *Heavy Matter: Urban Operations' Density of Challenges,* Santa Monica, CA: RAND, MR-1239-JS/A, 2000. More information on weapons deployment considerations in urban areas will be included in the next chapter, which covers the battlefield's effects. Information on weapons deployment is also found in Ralph Ellefson, *Urban Terrain Zone Characteristics,* Aberdeen Proving Ground, MD: U.S. Army Engineering Laboratory, 1987; Marine Corps Intelligence Activity, MCIA-1586-005-99, *Urban Generic Information Requirements Handbook,* Quantico, VA: United States Marine Corps, December 1998; and FM 5-33, *Terrain Analysis,* Washington, D.C.: Department of the Army, July 1998. For more information on considerations for C2, see Sean J.A. Edwards, *Freeing Mercury's Wings: Improving Tactical Communications in Cities,* Santa Monica, CA: RAND, MR-1316-A, 2001.

cultural awareness is essential to helping a planner or operator better see the city as its residents understand it. An educated perspective assists in identifying key features of the population and terrain. What are the defining social characteristics? Do the apparent instruments of control (police, politicians) represent the people or some other interest group? How are the neighborhoods configured? Are they segregated by physical or ethnic boundaries? What are the true sources of power and influence in the area of concern? Answers to these kinds of questions will lead to better understanding of how the military force can achieve its desired ends.

The example of the 1992 Los Angeles riots (see Figure 4.1) highlights the need to understand social as well as physical infrastructure characteristics. Table 4.1 provides several sample questions that might be asked during the AO and AOI definition processes to avoid the difficulties that military units unwittingly imposed on themselves in Los Angeles. The Marine Corps Intelligence Activity's *Urban Generic Information Requirements Handbook (GIRH)* includes other questions of potential value during analysis for the first step of the IPB process.

The 1992 Los Angeles Riots

At the beginning of the Los Angeles riots, military units drew AO boundaries to correspond to the city's freeways, features easily identified on both maps and the actual ground. This seemingly logical method was fundamentally flawed, however. Freeways are major *physical* features, but ones of limited *social* influence. While they may physically divide neighborhoods, this does not mean that those population segments residing on either side of the asphalt suffer disassociation. Local law enforcement agencies are aware of this phenomenon and have jurisdictional boundaries that reflect their understanding. Thus in choosing freeways to bound its units, the military crossed multiple police, fire, and other precinct or district borders. Command and control requirements were far more complicated than would have been the case had area of operation designations been made after coordination with the appropriate civilian agencies. These problems were quickly rectified by the redefinition of the original areas of operation.

SOURCE: James Delk, *Fires and Furies: The Los Angeles Riots of 1992.*

Figure 4.1—Designating the Urban AO

Table 4.1

Some Relevant Questions for Defining the AO and AOI

- What types of buildings are in the proposed AO?

- What is the interrelationship between the infrastructure in the proposed AO and that in other operational areas?

- Are there clear demographic boundaries that have a greater influence on mission success than do readily identifiable physical boundaries?

- How can the AO be defined to ease coordination between the unit and representatives of key demographic or governmental groups?

- How are demographic groups structured within the AO?

- Are there unique or culturally salient buildings within the area of concern?

- Are there particular buildings or areas that are currently contested among different demographic groups?

- Are there significant streets, avenues, or boulevards that contain key buildings of government, religious, or cultural interest?

It is apparent that the most militarily relevant elements in a city might not be its major structures or physical infrastructure. Designation of the urban AO, therefore, must consider the unknowns associated with an initial lack of intelligence of an area. It may contain far less obvious but more influential factors, such as religious activities conducted annually, monthly, daily, or even several times a day. The command staff must make every effort to see the city not only from friendly and enemy perspectives, but also from those of its residents.

Additionally, the vertical character of the AO, indeterminable via overhead imagery, could dramatically influence helicopter operations. Pending determination of whether rotary-wing support is feasible, an assigned AO may have to be drawn to include additional ground-level lines of communication. Recognizing what is unknown and adapting guidance to units based on these gaps in information are fundamental to the effectiveness of the ever-ongoing IPB process.

URBAN AREA(S) OF INTEREST

Urban AOI are geographic and temporal areas from which informa-tion and intelligence are required to plan and execute successful operations.[3] Traditional IPB usually limits the AOI to geographical areas from which the threat has the ability to jeopardize friendly force mission accomplishment.[4] Urban AOI must encompass more than this. As discussed in the previous chapter, urban architecture, social and physical infrastructure, and populations are entities linked by physical, economic, political, social, and cultural ties. The delin-eation of urban AOI must consider how these many links can influ-ence mission accomplishment within the AO.

Building design and physical infrastructure may influence AOI def-inition. Street layout, line of sight (LOS) into and out of the AO, and subterranean access are three possible considerations of importance. Designation of nodal AOI (those noncontiguous to the AO) may also be warranted. Monitoring local fire stations, police headquarters, religious centers, and the like could provide information on civil readiness and pending crises. Information on such areas could also explain what might mistakenly appear to be activities of potential concern, such as sudden movements of large numbers of the indige-nous population due to a pending sports event.

Urban infrastructure more clearly demonstrates the need to consider geographically distant or disconnected components of the AOI. Electrical wires, water treatment and supply systems, and media outlets are among the elements to consider. Is the electricity used within the AO generated in a distant area? Are there other means of energy transmission? Is electricity necessary for mission accom-

---

[3]This definition is from FM 101-5-1/MCRP 5-2.2 (DRAG Edition), *Operational Terms and Graphics,* Washington, D.C.: Department of the Army and Headquarters, United States Marine Corps, July 31, 1996, p. 1-17. The authors have added the phrase "and temporal" to the doctrinal definition.

[4]The most recent edition of FM 34-130/MCRP 2-12A, *Intelligence Preparation of the Battlefield (Coordinating Draft),* expands on the elements to be considered when delineating the AOI. Prior editions of the manual almost exclusively limit AOI designation to threat capabilities. See also Joint Pub 1-02, *Department of Defense Dictionary of Military and Associated Terms,* Washington, D.C.: Office of the Chairman, The Joint Chiefs of Staff, March 23, 1994, as amended through April 6, 1999, p. 37.

plishment? Are there antennas or transmission elements outside of the AO that can influence those within it?

Population groups complicate AOI definition not only because of their widespread interrelationships, but also because of their mobility. Citizens residing in the AO may move to another area for reasons as straightforward as commuting to work or for less savory purposes that have significant mission implications. Nongovernmental organizations (NGOs) or private volunteer organizations (PVOs) may deliberately or inadvertently influence noncombatant actions in ways that could likewise concern a military force. These organizations' activities are the result of decisions made both locally and at headquarters that may be thousands of miles distant. There may be a need to monitor these decisions if they could impact friendly force operations. Insurgent groups, organized crime elements, and other potential threats may receive support from diaspora or other entities in networks that channel funds, weapons, or other resources to groups within the AO. Recognizing and monitoring such relationships could be critical to both local operations and those distant from the AO.

The presence of media is also important to consider when delineating the AOI. Television, radio signals, the Internet, and other forms of media can all connect the AO with nonadjacent outside areas. The media can affect the information operations component of any mission as critically as the physical component. Being able to identify means of transmission and possible audiences to any kind of mission becomes a key component of defining an AOI for an urban operation.

Obviously the scope of influences pertinent to a unit's mission can potentially overwhelm its limited information-collection and processing capabilities. Barring the addition of supplemental assets, commanders and their staffs will have to focus on issues of notable importance while relegating the others to a lower priority. Ultimately the discrimination will depend on two questions:

- Could the issue under consideration influence actions in the AO so as to demonstrably affect mission accomplishment?

- If so, how?

Answering these questions will assist in identifying second- and higher-order effects of decisions and actions, a key element in properly defining the AOI.

URBAN BATTLESPACE

As defined earlier, the battlespace is "the conceptual physical volume in which the commander seeks to dominate the enemy. It expands and contracts in relation to the commander's ability to acquire and engage the enemy, or can change as the commander's vision of the battlefield changes."[5] The battlespace normally includes the AO and may include all or part of the AOI. Significantly, the battlespace also includes the areas or groups that can be influenced by events occurring within the AO. Its effects are therefore in a sense the reverse of those of concern when defining the AOI—which includes areas and other entities that can affect operations within the AO.

The key to distinguishing between the AOI and the battlespace is thus one of direction of cause and effect. The AOI Is composed of elements that can affect operations within the AO; the battlespace is composed of the areas (or personnel) that are affected by ongoing operations within the AO. What each of these areas is called when drawn on a map is less important than the outcome of the analysis that the concepts drive. Viewing the mission from the two-sided perspective of AOI and battlespace is notably valuable in an urban area, where the interconnectedness of its many parts guarantees numerous and complex interactions that must be understood during operations.

CHARACTERIZING RELEVANT FEATURES OF THE OPERATIONAL AREA AND IDENTIFYING INTELLIGENCE REQUIREMENTS

Determining the relevant characteristics of an urban operational area appears daunting given the amount of information to consider. Describing a city in general terms is difficult; attempting to highlight the features that are most salient to accomplishing the mission is

---

[5]FM 101-5-1/MCRP 5-2.2 (DRAG Edition), *Operational Terms and Graphics*, p. 1-33.

even more imposing. Two complementary approaches are suggested for managing this seemingly overwhelming task. The first is based on a density analysis of selected points within the urban AO, AOI, and battlespace.[6] The second approach devotes attention to analyzing relationships that exist between the primary components of a city: buildings, infrastructure, and population groups and the underlying terrain.

Density analysis provides a means of characterizing and assigning a relative importance to an urban area's heterogeneous elements. For example,

> if a town has many wells with potable water within its limits, chances are that sources of usable water will not rate designation as critical points. If, however, the number of water sources is low and the quantity of users high, one or more of those sources will likely merit critical point status.[7]

It might not always be the case that low density is tantamount to critical point. A high density of people at a street market on a given day might also be considered a critical point. The idea of density analysis is based on the relative worth of a single category of elements, compared to others of relevance in the operational area.

The second approach to determining what information is most critical is to identify the mission-salient relationships between elements that have been singled out as notably relevant. Population groups require the shelter of buildings, water, and (in some regions during parts of the year) heat. Infrastructure demands maintenance by individuals qualified to keep facilities in working order. Some groups depend on others for financial, emotional, medical, or other support. These various dependencies can be a source of productive relations or causes of instability. Beginning to understand which relationships are most important enables the identification of issues relevant to fulfilling intelligence requirements. For instance, an investigation into the South Central area of Los Angeles requires knowledge of

---

[6]This idea is fully explained in an article by Russell W. Glenn, *Urban Combat Is Complex*, Santa Monica, CA: RAND, RP-1001, 2002, and in Glenn, *Heavy Matter: Urban Operations' Density of Challenges*.

[7]Glenn, *Urban Combat Is Complex.*

what gangs are in the neighborhood, which of them have alliances or truces with each other or others outside South Central, which streets they control, and what kind of tagging (spray painting) each conducts. Understanding that these types of relationships are worthy of investigation is a major step in properly allocating intelligence assets.

Step one of urban IPB encompasses greater scope and complexity than is the norm for operations conducted in other environments. A disciplined approach, cultural and social awareness, and intellectual flexibility are all invaluable in effectively delineating the AO, AOI, and battlespace.

Chapter Five

IPB FOR URBAN OPERATIONS STEP TWO: DESCRIBE THE OPERATING ENVIRONMENT'S EFFECTS

I guess I expected our intel folks to know down to the minute who was who, what was what, and where [the enemy] was. I realize now how unrealistic that was of me, but at the time I didn't know what I didn't know.

Matt Eversmann,
discussing operations in 1993 Mogadishu[1]

The purpose of IPB step two is to describe the operational area in order to (1) acquaint the soldier with the environment he will inhabit during his upcoming mission, and (2) to help the unit staff determine how these surroundings will affect friendly and threat operations. Doctrinally, the second step of IPB is intended to describe how the existing conditions within the AO, AOI, and battlespace can affect friendly and enemy courses of action (COAs).[2] This is done by first identifying the existing conditions of the battlefield—the terrain, weather, and "other" conditions—and then describing how these conditions could possibly affect unit operations. For instance, terrain obstacles are identified early in the step. Subsequent analysis determines how these obstacles will influence a unit's operations.

Current IPB doctrine is devoted to helping intelligence and operations staffs describe environments that bear little resemblance to a U.S. soldier's urban, suburban, or rural home. Other terrain types,

---

[1] Matt Eversmann, interviewed by author, Santa Monica, California, May 23, 2000.

[2] FM 34-130/MCRP 2-12A, *Intelligence Preparation of the Battlefield,* Washington, D.C.: Department of the Army, July 1984.

such as jungles, deserts, and other less-populated areas, receive the majority of doctrinal attention. The terrain types currently addressed in doctrine are relatively easy to evaluate using the language of military terrain. Cover and concealment fit prescribed norms; avenues of approach are fairly identifiable; selecting key terrain is, more often than not, reasonably straightforward. Importantly, the enemy in these areas is often easily identified, and noncombatants are rarely present.

Urbanized areas, the terrain type in which many future U.S. military operations will occur, are less amenable to description using traditional military terminology and symbols. Although jungles and deserts vary, their degree of heterogeneity cannot compete with that of the world's villages, towns, and cities. Built-up areas of significant size will vary widely in their density of structures, lines of sight, density of occupants, width of avenues, and myriad other characteristics. This diversity creates uncertainty on how units and material can be deployed. Additionally, noncombatants are usually prevalent in urban areas, clouding identification of friend or foe and effectively dispelling the idea that they can be relegated to the "other" category when describing the battlefield's effects.

U.S. Army doctrine has begun to address some of the analytic challenges apparent in IPB step two. For instance, several doctrinal publications, including FM 5-33, *Terrain Analysis*, FM 34-130, *Intelligence Preparation of the Battlefield*, MCWP 3-35.3, *Military Operations on Urbanized Terrain*, FM 90-10, FM 90-10-1, and the Marine Corps *Urban Generic Information Requirements Handbook (GIRH)*, include discussions on how an urban landscape—its layout and construction—can influence military operations in urban areas. Street patterns, building function, construction materials, weapons effects, and LOS analyses are but a sampling of the considerations included in these manuals.[3]

---

[3]All of these manuals, the USMC *GIRH* in particular, include many ideas on how to assess and visualize the challenge of urban areas. Limitations of space keep us from including all of the relevant ideas in this report. It is suggested, however, that the interested reader refer to these manuals for further guidance in conducting IPB for MOUT.

FM 34-7, *IEW for Stability Operations and Support Operations* (Initial Draft), expands on currently doctrinal IPB step two by introducing methods of population analysis as part of an augmented approach to describing an operational area. FM 34-7, as well as the Marine Corps *Urban GIRH*, provides lists of factors that cover an area's demographics, history, culture, social and economic organization, government structure, and other pertinent factors often overlooked in traditional IPB.

The emphasis that FM 34-7 and the *Urban GIRH* put on population considerations for all types of operations is an important first step in addressing the variety of ways noncombatants can affect ongoing operations. People have the capability to affect an operation tactically, operationally, and strategically. These capabilities are enhanced in an urban environment where people are not only more numerous, but also have key assets of warfighting and information operations at hand. Consider Mogadishu, Somalia in 1992, where the effects of populations within the AO helped to defeat U.S. troops in a mission to capture Mohamed Farrah Aidid. Additionally, people within and outside of an AO brought about the hastened withdrawal of U.S. troops in the area. For instance, noncombatants and unarmed combatants present during a firefight contributed to the failure of a critical U.S. mission by helping combatants identify U.S. soldiers and providing human shields for the combatants. Another section of the population located within the AO, servicemen of different countries operating as part of a UN force, did not always cooperate with American players. People behind cameras in the same Mogadishu streets broadcast the aftermath of the firefight around the globe, affecting the American public's perception of the events. People in the United States, including the President, were appalled by the broadcasted scenes and demanded a withdrawal from Mogadishu.

Military operations on any terrain should include consideration of the natural topography, man-made structures and infrastructure, and the human population occupying the ground. People need to be protected, sustained, scrutinized, and influenced by the friendly unit. Additionally, people might influence activities in a specific location within a city where a unit might be deployed. For instance, a population within a particular area of a city might be more sympathetic to an adversary's cause and provide safe houses for members of the opposing force. In a support mission, one sector of a city might suffer greater devastation during a natural disaster than another. Realizing the specific needs of that sector of the city, while trying to accommodate the requirements of the population in other areas, requires an understanding of all population components of the city.

Because of a population's ability to affect a military operation in a variety of ways, it is suggested that the intelligence analyst conducting IPB for urban operations should place a primary focus on the city's inhabitants. With a better understanding of the people who drive urban activity, analysis of other urban features such as building and infrastructure can be better focused to address the unit's mission and the needs of the people. For the aforementioned reasons, the authors describe the population analysis of urban IPB step two, *describe the environment's effects,* first.

As with the other suggestions presented in this work, the recommendations and ideas that follow are meant either to inform the intelligence or operations staff of the tools already available for assessing urban dilemmas, or to introduce new tools that can be used independently or together to help with mission planning. The following suggestions are not meant to replace existing doctrine, merely to augment it. In fact, using all the suggested products might prove overwhelming for an already overburdened staff. It is worth noting that many of the products listed in this chapter are already in use by Army and Marine Corps staffs. Many other products are also in use but not listed in this report. Interested readers are referred to the doctrine listed in the bibliography for further investigation of extant intelligence and mission-planning products.

POPULATION ANALYSIS

> Accommodating the social fabric of a city is potentially the most influential factor in the conduct of urban operations. . . . The fastest way to damage the legitimacy of an operation is to ignore or violate social mores or precepts of a particular population.
>
> Marine Corps Intelligence Activity
> *Urban Generic Information Requirements Handbook*

> The greatest challenge to operational IPB is the analysis of the human factors. Clausewitz's trinity of the nation-state: government, army and people; places the emotion of passion which fans the flames of "primordial violence, hatred and enmity" in the corner of the people.
>
> William F. Grimsley
> *Intelligence Preparation of the Future Operational Battlefield*

Cities exist because of the people living within them. They are "centers of finance, politics, transportation, communications, industry and culture, [that] generally have large population[s]."[4] Although typically considered true only for MOOTW, "the density of civilians and the constant interaction between them and U.S. forces greatly increases the importance of social considerations."[5] It is with this in mind that we begin discussion of urban IPB step two with an analysis of the people residing in urban areas.

Any discussion of a city's population requires a two-pronged approach. Developing a clear picture of a city's population requires delineating its primary attributes, such as age, wealth, gender, ethnicity, religion, and employment statistics. Collecting this information and reporting its significance is considered *demographic analysis*. The second component, *cultural intelligence*, describes the process by which cultural information—food preferences, mores, values, relationships and rivalries between particular groups, to name a few—is incorporated with demographic information to uncover the underlying characteristics of the population that the unit will face. Demographic analysis describes *what* conditions exist. Cultural intelligence is devoted to describing *why* conditions exist. Techniques for assisting in both of these tasks are described in the next section.

---

[4]Marine Corps Intelligence Activity, *Urban Generic Information Requirements Handbook*, MCIA-1586-005-99, December 1998.

[5]Ibid.

Demographic Analysis and Cultural Intelligence

Cultural intelligence has many manifestations, but its central purpose. . .
is to bridge the chasm from perceiving, and thus reacting to, the world as
random and inexplicable to understanding the world as eminently know-
able, and hence being able to act in concert with reality.

Dorothy A. Geyer
Seminar on cultural intelligence

Some societies are governed by the rule of law, others by the rule of men.
Some by religious/local tradition, and others by the tradition or customs
of a clan.

Timothy Thomas
Some Asymmetric Lessons of Urban Combat:
The Battle for Grozny

Demographic analysis seeks to characterize population groups and
subgroups within a commander's entire area of concern. Both the
Marine Corps *Urban GIRH* and Army FM 34-7 provide useful check-
lists of the factors that should be considered when conducting
demographic analysis. Using these lists, the analyst can create pictures—often in the form of templates, overlays, or descriptions—of a
city's key societal characteristics. Examples of some of the products
that are already used by the armed services are listed in Table 5.1.[6]
These demographic tools show how the population "looks on paper."
They delineate the critical factors that define each population group
and show where differences exist, and they are readily available to
intelligence analysts and command staff members.

But these tools also generate a picture of a city based on static information. They do not necessarily describe the population as a thinking component of the operational area, nor do they attribute any
type of dynamism or reactiveness to the people. Often, operational
planning might require a more in-depth understanding of the population. How demographic traits influence the population's actions,

---

[6]Many of the products listed in the tables in this chapter are available to soldiers as
they are deployed but are not a part of formal doctrine as of this writing.

Table 5.1

Existing Demographic Analysis Products for IPB

Population status overlay

This product depicts how the population of a designated area is divided based on a single characteristic such as age, religion, ethnicity, or income. For instance, one population status overlay can show what areas of a city are Catholic, Protestant, Muslim, Hindu, and so on. Another overlay can indicate income levels or areas of known gang membership. There is no limit to the number of overlays that can be created to depict the population characteristics of a chosen area. The benefits of these overlays range from determining possible lines of contention (that can exist between groups) or identification of the population/location in greatest need of a certain activity or asset. Many of this type of overlay are produced by the United Nations High Commission for Refugees and are readily available on its web site.[a]

Congregation points overlay

Congregation points such as places of religious worship, parks, schools, restaurants, squares, recreational centers, sports facilities, or entertainment centers can be indicated on maps of a city. These locations can also be coded with information on the population group that frequents them, days and hours of operation, and type of activity that occurs.

Nocturnal conditions, diurnal conditions

Part of the U.S. ability to "own the night" depends on who else is contending for it. Population dispersal can vary significantly throughout the day. An overlay indicating the location of population groups during the day, and how this changes over time, might help identify possibly restrictive operating conditions or reveal times that are most conducive for completion of a given mission.

Building type overlay

The building type overlay can depict particular types of buildings, such as government buildings, religious centers, or media locations. Each of the buildings can be numbered or otherwise identified depending on the needs of the commander and his staff. Additionally, entire sections of a city can be marked depending on the construction type prevalent in a particular area. For instance, an area of dense construction or a shantytown can be identified by appropriately labeling it on an overlay or directly onto an aerial photograph.

Table 5.1—continued

Traffic conditions, times and locations

"[A]irborne surveillance could easily detect a traffic jam but it would provide little indication or prediction as to why and when it would occur or whether it were a routine or exceptional event."[b] A description of normal traffic conditions can help the unit determine best times to operate. It can also provide an indicator of an exceptional event.

Overlay of most likely threat locations

Because "enemy fighters in the city can be in the windows of any floor of any building, yards away with a large weapon, or the seemingly innocent man in the street who is hired to kill . . . emphasis may be placed on those elements that provide the adversary the ability to occupy certain areas."[c] In Northern Ireland for instance, it was often helpful for the Royal Ulster Constabulary (RUC) to know what areas housed those that were sympathetic to the Irish Republican Army (IRA). Having this information allowed them to determine where the members of the IRA might be meeting or hiding weapons. The RUC also used its connections within IRA sympathetic neighborhoods to determine why certain neighborhoods were supporting the IRA cause.[d]

---

[a]See *http://www.reliefweb.com* for examples of this type of template.

[b]Fritz J. Barth, "The Urban Awareness Concept," *The MOUT Homepage, http://www.geocities.com/Pentagon/6453/urbanawareness.html.*

[c]Marine Corps Intelligence Activity, *Urban Generic Information Requirements Handbook*, MCIA-1586-005-99, December 1998.

[d]For a good discussion on how the RUC sought to understand the sympathies of Northern Ireland neighborhoods, see Charles Allen, *The Savage Wars of Peace: Soldiers' Voices 1945–1989*, London: Michael Joseph, 1990.

expectations, and relationships with other groups within the area of operation, associated area of interest, and battlespace might be critical to maintaining stability within the host city. This information might also prove useful in establishing legitimacy or obtaining allegiance from populations during low-intensity operations. It is exceptionally critical for any type of information operation; without cultural understanding, information operations might be completely ineffective. The example from Northern Ireland provided in Figure 5.1 reflects how understanding a culture means more than knowing

[T]alk to everybody, keep talking, keep a smile on your face, always laugh . . . and it worked. We made lots of friends and we established a link with both communities on either side of what had now been called the "peace line," which was a long barricade . . . [that] had been constructed to stop the so-called "marauding gangs" of hooligans coming up from the Catholic side and setting light to more Protestant houses and equally to stop the marauding gangs from the Protestant side.

SOURCE: Charles Allen, *The Savage Wars of Peace: Soldiers' Voices 1945–1989.*

Figure 5.1—Developing Cultural Intelligence in Northern Ireland

what part of town the unit is patrolling; it means making a concerted effort to know the habits, likes, and dislikes of the neighborhood's inhabitants. It is this type of understanding that *cultural intelligence* products seek to provide. Cultural intelligence describes how the population looks "in practice." It augments demographic analysis by describing how demographic traits and relationships between groups can act, or have already acted, to stabilize or destabilize conditions. Some cultural intelligence tools are listed in Table 5.2. Most of these tools are already discussed in currently available doctrine or other lessons-learned materials. Where appropriate, those tools being newly introduced (or at least believed to be so) are indicated as such.

Below we introduce two additional cultural intelligence products that seek to assist in developing a deeper understanding of how the population within the operational area can actively affect the ongoing operation. Both are dynamic tools—they should be constantly updated to measure changing conditions. These products are also introduced in very simplified form, for use in any type of operation. They can be modified, refined, augmented, and automated to suit the more sophisticated needs of intelligence or law enforcement agencies.

Table 5.2

Sample Cultural Intelligence Products for Urban IPB

Lists and timelines of salient cultural and political events

For some operations, a list of key holidays of the host nation (HN) is provided to the deployed soldier in order to forewarn him of possibly increased or unusual activity on given dates. These lists, however, rarely include a description of why these dates are significant and what can be expected to happen on the holiday. *Timelines*—a list of significant dates along with relevant information and analysis—seek to provide a context to operational conditions. These timelines could include descriptions of population movements or political shifts that are relevant to the operational area. They could also include a brief historical record of the population or area, highlighting the activities of a certain population sector. As analytic tools, timelines might help the intelligence analyst predict how key sectors of the population might react to given circumstances.

Culture description or cultural comparison chart or matrix

"It has been demonstrated repeatedly that foreign countries do not always respond as we predict. Though frequently labeled 'crazy,' it is more likely that they have applied different values in arriving at their solutions to problems. Organizations will allocate resources based on their values and beliefs."[a] In order for the intelligence analyst to avoid the common mistake of assuming that only one perspective exists, it may be helpful to clearly point out the extant ideology, politics, predominant religion, acceptable standards of living, and mores. A *culture comparison chart* can be a stand-alone tool, just listing the different characteristics of the culture in question, or it can be comparative—assessing the HC population relative to known and familiar conditions. Currently, soldiers being deployed to a foreign operational area are provided little more than descriptions of the most relevant cultural characteristics they will encounter.

Line of confrontation overlay or matrix

The overlays and descriptions resulting from assessing the demographic characteristics of the host city population might reveal significant differences between groups. These unfriendly relationships can be highlighted and mapped on a *Line of Confrontation overlay*. The Royal Ulster Constabulary described their operational area in terms of how its demographic composition created possible cleavage points. As Charles Allen describes in his account of the low-intensity conflict in Northern Ireland, "In both Belfast and Londonderry the barricades had gone up and a series of 'no-go' enclaves had been created. . . . In Londonderry the population was predomnately Catholic, concentrated in the districts of

Table 5.2—continued

Creggan, Brandywell and Bogside on the western side of the River Foyle. In Belfast, however, the Protestants were in the majority. . . . As far as those in the Army were concerned they went into Belfast and Londonderry not just to keep the warring communities apart but also to protect the minority community."[b]

Culturally significant structures overlay

This product highlights places of religious worship (e.g., churches, temples, mosques), all relevant government buildings and internationally significant build-ings (e.g., embassies, consulates), and other structures or areas of notable cultural importance.

"Power" templates (Newly Introduced)

This template can include what type of influence a group wields (economic, armed, political), how groups are interlinked, and what the strength is of each group within the categories. For instance, the influence of organized crime can be charted by showing what type of influence and over whom the criminal group wields it.

Status quo ante bellum overlay (SQABO) and/or a series of overlays that can be animated with the use of a CD-ROM (Newly Introduced)

Similar to the timeline of salient events, status quo ante bellum products describe the history and potential underpinnings of the current instability. They can also provide instructive analysis of past circumstances that can affect the outcome of the current mission. For instance, a SQABO for a disaster relief operation could include coverage of how the population was situated prior to the disaster as well as historical examples of how the recovery mission for a past disaster was conducted. When used for a SASO or combat mission, the SQABO can show population shifts, resource movements, or increased violence that are the result of a historical or dramatic event. Each overlay should depict some status quo condition at a disclosed time period. The overlays produced should be compared to significant changes in the environment or a relevant event. This comparison will demonstrate how the population has responded to each significant event and might help the analyst determine a COA that will help regain stability in the area.

[a]John B. Alexander, *Future War: Non-Lethal Weapons in Twenty-First-Century Warfare*, New York: St. Martin's Press, 1999.

[b]Charles Allen, *The Savage Wars of Peace: Soldiers' Voices 1945–1989.* London: Michael Joseph, 1990.

Relationship matrices (Newly Introduced). Relationship matrices are intended to depict the nature of relationships between elements of the operational area. The elements can include members from the noncombatant population, the friendly force, international organizations, and an adversarial group. Utility infrastructure, significant buildings, and media might also be included. The nature of the relationship between two or more components includes measures of contention, collusion, or dependency. The purpose of this product is to demonstrate graphically how each component of the city interacts with the others and whether these interactions promote or degrade the likelihood of mission success. The relationships represented in the matrix can also begin to help the analysts in deciphering how to best use the relationship to help shape the environment.

The example relationship matrix shown in Figure 5.2, while not complete, is intended to show how the relationships among a representative compilation of population groups can be depicted. This example is an extremely simple version of what might be used during an operation in which many actors and other population elements are present. For instance, the section marked "Population" might include considerably more population subgroups than the two included in this sample. When used during a deployment, it is important for the analysts to realize what groups, subgroups. and other elements should be represented in the matrix. In addition, it should be noted that the matrix could be used to depict the perceived differences in relationships. For example, in the sample matrix below, political group 3 is shown to have a dependent relationship with economic group 1. The complementary relationship (a similar mark in the corresponding box linking political group 3 and economic group 1) is not indicated because it might not exist.

To illustrate the usefulness of the matrix, consider the relationship of the government with the infrastructure. In this case, the relationship is "friendly," perhaps because the government is in control of the infrastructure without contest from the owners or suppliers of the infrastructure. Such could be considered the case when Slobodan Milosevic controlled the electricity supply for Kosovo. He apparently used the infrastructure at his disposal to supply electricity to the population, but intermittently threatened to deny the service in order to maintain control over a possibly hostile population. How

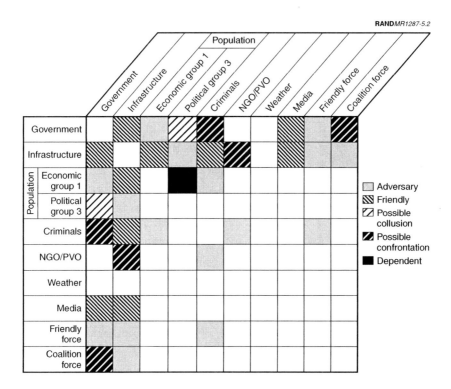

Figure 5.2—Sample Relationship Matrix

can this information be used by the commander and his staff? Perhaps by understanding the nature of two components on the battlefield, the link between the two elements can either be eliminated or leveraged in order to suit the needs of the friendly unit.

Using the same matrix, there is a relationship of possible collusion that exists between the government and political group 3, and a friendly relationship between the government and the media. The questions the intelligence analyst might ask when reviewing this information include: How can the government use the media to its advantage? Will the government seek to discredit political group 3 using the media? Will the population view the media's reporting as credible? Does the population see the government as willfully using the media to suit its own ends?

Legitimacy is a condition based on the perception by a specific audience of the legality, morality or rightness of a set of actions. . . . If an operation is not perceived as legitimate, the actions may not be supported and may be actively resisted.

Joint Publication 3-07
Joint Doctrine for Military Operations Other Than War

Perception Assessment Matrices (Newly Introduced). "Perception is the interpretation of sensory input from seeing, hearing, smelling, tasting or touching. Perception is also influenced by physiological capacities, frames of reference, learning, past experiences, and cultural and social environments."[7] Friendly force activities intended to be benign or benevolent might have negative results if a population's perceptions are not first investigated and subsequently measured or managed. This is true because *perceptions*—more than reality—drive decisionmaking and in turn could influence the reactions of entire populations. The perception assessment matrix seeks to provide some measure of effectiveness for the unit's ability to maintain legitimacy during an operation. In this sense, the matrix can also be used to directly measure the effectiveness of the unit's CA, PA, and PSYOP efforts.[8]

One proposed PSYOP campaign developed for Operation RESTORE DEMOCRACY in Haiti might prove illustrative of why perception assessment is necessary. Prior to deployment, leaflets were published informing the Haitian populace of U.S. intentions. The original leaflet was published in Dutch, the language of the Haitian elite. The one actually used for the PSYOP campaign was published in Creole, the official language of Haiti, because an astute PSYOP team member realized the need to publish to the wider audience. If the Dutch flier had been dropped on Port-au-Prince, it could have undermined the American mission to the country in several ways. The majority of the population would have been unable to read the flier. The subsequent deployment of U.S. forces into the country there-

---

[7]FM 33-1-1, *Psychological Operations Techniques and Procedures,* Washington D.C.: Department of the Army, 1994.

[8]The reader is directed to FM 33-1-1 for more information on perception assessment and its role in information operations, particularly PSYOP. See also FM 3-05.3, *Psychological Operations,* Washington, D.C.: Department of the Army, 2000.

fore, could have been perceived to be hostile. The mission itself, which was intended in part to restore equity within the nation's social structure, could have backfired if the Haitians viewed the Dutch flier as an indication of U.S. favoritism to the Haitian elite.

Perception can work counter to operational objectives. Perceptions should therefore be assessed both before and throughout an operation. Although it is not possible to read the minds of the HC population, there are several means to measure its perceptions.

1. Demographic analysis and cultural intelligence are key components of perception analysis.

2. Understanding a population's history can help predict expectations and reactions.

3. HUMINT can provide information on population perceptions.

4. Reactions and key activities can be carefully observed in order to decipher whether people act based on real conditions or perceived conditions.

5. Editorial and opinion pieces of relevant newspapers can be monitored for changes in tone or opinion shifts that can steer or may be reacting to the opinions of a population group.

Perception assessment matrices aim to measure the disparities between friendly force actions and what population groups perceive. A sample matrix is provided in Figure 5.3.

In addition to trying to assess the perceptions of each population group within an operational area, it might serve the interests of the unit to assess its own perceptions of its activities. Are members of the unit exhibiting decidedly Western or American values that are not appreciated by the HC population? Are embedded American beliefs preventing the unit from understanding the HC population or its coalition partners? Is what the intelligence and command staff is perceiving really what is going on in the operational area? Does the population believe what the unit believes? Is there something that is part of the population's (or a subgroup's) perception that can be detrimental to the unit? All these questions can begin to be addressed by the unit's scrutinizing its view of an operation.

Condition	Cultural norm	Alternative proposed by friendly force	Population's perception	Acceptable difference?	Root of difference	Possible to change?	Proposed solution	Possible consequences of not changing
Food	Rice	Meat and potatoes	Inadequate/ inconsiderate	No	Cultural proclivity, no known physically detrimental effects	No; logistically restricted	Just offer potatoes, seek exchange for rice	Starvation, rioting
Use of guns	All men carry weapons	All weapons confiscated	Unfair	No	Culture	No; soldier safety	PSYOP campaign; just weapon search	Armed backlash
Government structure	Tribal	Hierarchical	Tolerable as long as needs are fulfilled by group in charge	Yes	History	No	Bargain	Unknown

Figure 5.3—Perception Assessment Matrix: Perceptions of the Host City Population

Assessing the OCOKA Factors of the Population (Newly Introduced)

Often a force deployed into an urban area will not have the time or the resources to conduct a complete demographic analysis and cultural intelligence picture before operations begin. In the absence of a complete intelligence picture, tactical operations might be assisted by the use of a familiar IPB tool: assessing the OCOKA factors of the operational area. OCOKA—observation and fields of fire, concealment and cover, obstacles, key terrain, and avenues of approach—can be applied to the population to evaluate how various groups within and outside of the AO will affect a unit's operation.

Using OCOKA to describe the ways the population can affect a mission is useful for operations on the ground as well as for information operations (IO). In terms of ground operations, any unit can adopt it as a method for communicating the ways in which the population affects maneuver, weapons use, and movement. For IO purposes, seeking to define the population in terms of OCOKA can help the intelligence analyst identify target audiences, develop the most effective means of communication, and measure the results of a chosen IO campaign. The population OCOKA factors listed in Table 5.3 include examples for both ground operations and information operations. Physical OCOKA effects are those that demonstrate how people can physically interfere or abet mission accomplishment. Information operations effects seek to describe how the population, as a thinking component of the operational area, will react to unit operations.

Figure 5.4 provides illustrative examples of how population OCOKA is similar to the familiar terrain OCOKA.

Table 5.3

Population OCOKA

Observation and fields of fire

- Individuals or groups in the population can be co-opted by one side or another to perform a *surveillance* or *reconnaissance* function, performing as moving outposts to gather information.

- City residents have intimate knowledge of the city. Their *observations* can provide information and insights about what might otherwise remain a mystery. For instance, residents often know about shortcuts through town. They might also be able to observe and report on a demonstration or meeting that occurs in their area.

- Unarmed combatants might provide targeting intelligence to armed combatants engaged in a confrontation. This was readily apparent in Mogadishu, where unarmed combatants with the ability to *observe* friendly force activities without the threat of being engaged instructed hidden threat forces on where to fire.

- Deception and adversarial PSYOP campaigns may *hinder a clear view* of the adversary's tactics or intentions.

- *Fields of fire* can be extremely limited by the presence of noncombatants in a combat zone because restrictive ROE may prohibit firing into a crowd.

- Figuratively, the population or sectors within a city can be targeted as *fields of fire* for information operations.

Concealment and cover

- Civilian populations provide ubiquitous *concealment* for nonuniformed forces. Threat forces operating in any part of a city can instantly blend into any type of crowd or activity.

- Adversaries often find *cover* from firepower by operating within a nonadversarial or neutral group. For instance, during the December 1999 World Trade Organization demonstrations in Seattle, organized, unruly, and dangerous protestors, "hid behind peaceful demonstrators, creating a situation where if [the Seattle police] were to be successful in countering their tactics, a larger number of people likely would have been hurt."[a]

- "Chechen rebels and the Hezbollah effectively used the *cover of refugees* to attack occupying forces and counted on heavy civilian casualties in the counterattack to gain support with the native population."[b] The support offered by the native population in this case provided a type of political cover that hindered Russian and Israeli operations.

Table 5.3—continued

- A particularly telling example of using the guise of noncombatants as cover is a story about the use of a woman by Amal fighters to reconnoiter Marine and LAF positions in Beirut between 1982 and 1984. "The most blatant of the scouts was a heavyset middle-aged woman—or large man dressed in a woman's clothing—who made trip after trip across the end of the alley. One of the Marine riflemen reached the end of his tether late in the afternoon and dropped her in her tracks with one M-16 round. An Amal gunman who was duck-walking on the woman's ample hidden side scuttled for a nearby building when his cover fell to the street."[c]

Obstacles

- One of the largest *obstacles* to friendly operations is the portion of the population that supports the adversary.

- People conducting their daily activities will simply "get in the way" of any type of operation. For instance, curiosity-driven crowds in Haiti often affected patrols by inadvertently forcing units into the middle of the street and pushing them into a single file. No harm was inflicted, but the unit was made more vulnerable to sniper and grenade attacks.

- Strategically the world audience, as well as its local contingent, can create *political, cultural, and ideological obstacles* to a mission. The American audience watching events unfold in Vietnam could have been perceived as an obstacle to the government's strategy of pursuing its strategic objectives. The cultural differences apparent when U.S. forces were deployed for Operation Desert Storm could have been an obstacle if not adequately addressed. For instance, a PSYOP flier produced to encourage a sense of unity among the Arab populations included a picture of two men holding hands—a sight not common in Western cultures. A flier designed in accordance with Western standards might not have been as effective.

Key terrain

- Instructional materials used at U.S. Army Intelligence Center and Fort Huachuca often label the *international audience* to an Army operation as "*key terrain*." The audience is assigned this designation based on the idea that public opinion can change the course or the aims of a mission. The U.S. withdrawal from Somalia following the American outcry after seeing a soldier being dragged through the streets of Mogadishu is often used in MOUT literature as an example of the power of an audience. Determining which population or portions of it are key to a mission should not be limited to broad-brush characterizations of large populations, however. Certain sectors or individuals within a population can be as pivotal in modern engagements as a piece of high ground was in bygone eras, or as the entire American population was in Mogadishu.

Table 5.3—continued

- Captured combatants or a well-informed noncombatant can provide valuable intelligence about the enemy. These individuals can be key terrain in terms of the intelligence they can provide.

- A group of people that U.S. forces are deployed to protect might be considered key terrain because loss of that group's respect could jeopardize the entire operation.

- Congregations of people can be considered key terrain. Whether moving or stationary, a large gathering might be a ripe target for attack, closer observation, or attempts at manipulation.

Avenues of approach

- Populations present during MOUT physically restrict movement and maneuver by limiting or changing the width of an AA.

- People may assist movement if a group can be used as human barriers between one combatant group and another. Refugee flows, for example can provide a concealed AA for members of a force.

- A certain individual can provide an AA to a specific target audience when acting as a mouthpiece for an information operation mission.

[a] Kim Murphy, "Anarchists Deployed New Tactics in Violent Seattle Demonstrations," *Los Angeles Times,* December 16, 1999.

[b] Marine Corps Intelligence Activity, *The Urban Century: Developing World Urban Trends and Possible Factors Affecting Military Operations,* MCIA-1586-003-98, November 1997. Emphasis added.

[c] Eric Hammel, *The Root: Marines in Beirut, August 1982–February 1984,* San Diego: Harcourt Brace Jovanovich, 1985.

Information Operations Analysis (Newly Introduced)

Four hostile newspapers are more to be feared than a thousand bayonets.

Napoleon Bonaparte

Media reporting influences public opinion, which may affect the perceived legitimacy of an operation and ultimately influence the success or failure of the operation.

Joint Publication 3-07
Joint Doctrine for Military Operations Other Than War

	Terrain OCOKA	Population OCOKA	
		Evaluation of Physical Effects	Evaluation of Information Effects
Observation and fields of fire	Hilltop	HUMINT, restricted use of weapons	HUMINT, target audience
Concealment and cover	Foliage	Noncombatants prohibit engagement	PSYOP and deception conceal intentions
Obstacles	Cliff	Noncombatants "get in the way"	Cultural differences impede understanding
Key terrain	Bridge	Crowd location	Critical leader
Avenues of approach	Open field	Crowds limit AAs	Audiences provide AA to hearts and minds

Figure 5.4—OCOKA for Terrain and Population, Examples

Information is a key component of any operation. It can instill legitimacy in a mission, create favorable conditions through PSYOP, or communicate a task. Understanding how information can affect an operation in terms of legitimacy and its use as a tool of warfare is essential in urban areas, an environment in which information is more readily available to large and varied audiences than in other environments.

Information transmitted through various media sources affects operations at all levels of war. At the strategic level, the media's influence on international and domestic public opinion can often change the course of an operation, legitimizing it or delegitimizing it depending on the information's source, content, and audience. The concept of the "strategic corporal" draws its origins from this phenomenon. A single decision made at the tactical level can potentially have decisive strategic effects.

Information can affect strategic decisions in a more direct way. Advanced technology and the prevalence of popular media sources (television, radio, newspapers, and the Internet) make more information available to military decisionmakers. This information may then be used in lieu of intelligence during the military decisionmaking process. This situation occurred during Operation Desert Storm:

high-ranking officials are said to have made decisions based on what they saw on television rather than on intelligence provided to them.[9]

The number of information sources in a city also increases the number of people communicating (or blocking the communication). At the tactical level, graffiti, fax machines, the Internet, light signals, and car horns are just a few examples of the many means of communication available to any city resident. The residents of Mogadishu, Somalia, used hand signals to designate targets for armed combatants.

Components of media analysis include sources, mediums, themes, and target audiences. *Sources* of information are those parties transmitting information. Source analysis requires investigation of who owns the resources used to transmit a message, what the stated or known position is, and the nature and extent of the resources available to the source.

Information *mediums* are the mechanisms used to transmit the message. They are essentially the "hardware" associated with message transmission. As such, they are probably the most easily identifiable and readily manipulated portion of information operations. Mediums include the obvious: radio, television, fax machines, and pamphlets. "Low-tech" means include walls that are susceptible to graffiti, runners, hand signals, and even burning tires. It is important to identify mediums (such as television, radio, and newspapers) that are typically considered most credible and useful to the population. For instance, the impact of the Implementation Force (IFOR) information campaign in Bosnia was limited because it was conducted with print and AM radio ads—but Bosnians preferred television and FM radio.[10]

A *theme* is a subject or line of persuasion used to achieve a psychological objective. Themes are often used in advertising to motivate a certain behavior. A sports drink commercial, for example, seeks to target those who are currently thirsty as well as those who might be thirsty in the future. The theme of "thirst" is used to convey the message that the drink product will quench the thirst whenever it occurs.

---

[9] Frank J. Stech, "Winning CNN Wars," *Parameters*, Autumn 1994, p. 37.

[10] Larry K. Wentz (ed.), *Lessons from Bosnia: The IFOR Experience*, Vienna, VA: CCRP, 1997.

Target audiences can also be evaluated based on their vulnerabilities, preconceptions, susceptibility to new information, interrelationships among groups, and identification of key leaders of these groups. Target audiences might be more greatly influenced by informal leaders, for example. This was the case in Operation Desert Shield and Desert Storm, in which a well-known celebrity was chosen for the "Voice of the Gulf" because he could appeal to a larger public audience than a government figure. Target audiences with the ability to influence or change the behavior of a larger group are potentially very valuable to a military commander. Current PSYOP doctrine discusses target audience evaluation in depth.

The *information source analysis matrix,* shown in Figure 5.5, is a conceptual tool that can be used to evaluate each information medium, source, and audience within a city. By filling in each of the cells with a descriptor, a staff can gain a good idea of how information is exchanged and used. Note that this tool can be used to assess opinion and editorial pieces from newspapers and television programs, in addition to its other uses. This can assist in the perception assessment analysis discussed earlier.

Non-U.S. Actor Analysis

> NGOs, PVOs, and [international organizations] have representatives in country before the military arrive, while the military are present, and after the military leave. They are important players that the military needs to be prepared to deal with in peace operations.
>
> Larry K. Wentz (ed.)
> *Lessons from Bosnia: The IFOR Experience*

Given the scope of U.S. alliances, the likelihood that U.S. forces will work side by side with the soldiers of other nations during any type of operation is virtually guaranteed. Humanitarian obligations also necessitate the presence of international aid organizations to assist the local populace. During domestic operations, including intercolonial territories, soldiers will work alongside local police officers, firemen, national guard troops, and other actors not inherent to their unit. These many nonorganic actors provide a mixed blessing for

RAND*MR1287-5.5*

Medium	Source					Audience		
	Content	Slant	Context	Frequency of coverage	Sponsor	Population sector	Receptivity	Reaction
Radio								
Frequency 1								
Frequency 2								
Frequency 3								
TV								
Channel 1								
Channel 2								
Channel 3								
Print								
Newspaper 1								
Newspaper 2								
Newspaper 3								
Word of mouth								
Source 1								
Source 2								
Source 3								
Internet								
Site 1								
Site 2								
Site 3								
Pamphlets								
Type 1								
Type 2								
Type 3								
Graffiti								
Type 1								
Type 2								
Type 3								

Figure 5.5—Information Source Analysis Matrix (Newly Introduced)

U.S. forces: they are bolstered by the assistance these groups provide and threatened by the possibility that a misunderstanding will further complicate what may already be an unstable environment.

Non-Army actors can be beneficial sources of host nation (HN) cultural information. During the 1999 fighting in Kosovo, the Red Cross provided the most accurate figures on the number of Kosovar refugees, helping U.S. and other coalition services to estimate the appropriate level of support required to handle their needs. Civilian agencies also "develop a network of influential contacts, compile historical and specialty archives, and establish relationships with local leaders and business people. They understand the infrastructure of the region, and the political and economic influences."[11] International aid organizations sometimes keep up-to-date web sites with maps and pertinent information on local and regional areas that could be of potential value to military planners.[12]

Partners in a coalition environment have different capabilities, procedures, doctrine, rules of engagement, and methods of disclosing information. These differences can be at once frustrating and useful. For instance, soldiers of the United Kingdom and United States working side by side in Bosnia had different methods of collecting and sharing intelligence. This frustrated intelligence analysts' ability to work as a cohesive group but provided HUMINT resources to the United States that would not otherwise have been available.

Non-U.S. actor analysis should seek to list all the key similarities and differences among all groups in an operational area. Population sta-

---

British power in India at this time consisted of two elements: the native armies of the East India Company and a comparatively few regular British Army units . . . . Due largely to poor administration and command, considerable unrest existed among native contingents. The introduction of the Minie rifle cartridge . . . provided the spark that changed unrest to violence. The paper cartridge, which had to be bitten for loading, was greased. Disaffected elements in the armies claimed . . . that the grease used included the fat of cows (sacred to Hindus) and of pigs (unclean to Mohammedans).

SOURCE: R. Ernest Dupuy and Trevor N. Dupuy, *The Encyclopedia of Military History: From 3500 B.C. to the Present.*

Figure 5.6—The Importance of Non-U.S. Actor Analysis

---

[11]Wentz, *Lessons from Bosnia.*

[12]For instance, see the web sites for USAID *(www.usaid.gov),* UN *(www.un.org),* and Reliefweb *(www.reliefweb.int).*

tus overlays or relationship matrices that contain categories like ROE, information-sharing capabilities, aid resources, and other pieces of relevant information can be constructed to evaluate each of the nonorganic actors the U.S. unit is dealing with. A relationship matrix focusing on how the United States relates to each nonorganic actor and ways in which those actors might pursue relationships with members of the HC population will also be helpful in determining how coalition members, PVOs, NGOs, the media, and other partici-pants could influence the mission. A matrix containing each NGO and PVO capabilities, location, and relationships will assist both operators and intelligence analysts.

The indigenous population, fellow coalition members, and other U.S. and non-Army actors involved in an urban operation will dramati-cally influence both the operational and intelligence aspects of a mission. This does not mean that traditional IPB factors, the terrain and weather, have less value in a built-up area. Modifications in their analysis will be needed to describe their effects. The uses of extant methods and some new ideas on terrain and weather analysis for urban IPB follow below.

URBAN TERRAIN ANALYSIS

> Unique to MOUT is that the conduct of operations can radically alter the physical nature of the terrain in ways not previously experienced nor encountered in other environments. Some buildings suffer damage with collapsed walls and roofs, while others are razed completely, leaving only a pile of rubble. These effects can be militarily significant, as some key terrain features completely disappear and fields of fire open and close.
>
> Marine Corps Intelligence Activity
> *Urban Generic Information Requirements Handbook*

Early editions of FM 34-130/MCRP 2-12A, *Intelligence Preparation of the Battlefield,* limit terrain analysis to investigation of the military aspects of terrain (OCOKA) and how these factors affect both threat and friendly operations. The diversity and density of man-made features in urban areas, superimposed on varying natural topogra-phy, pose overwhelming analytic challenges that may greatly com-

plicate OCOKA analysis. The man-made nature of the terrain intro-
duces three substantial difficulties for terrain analysis:

1. Structures hamper military operations in terms of maneuver:
   street width, building construction, subterranean and superter-
   ranean dimensions, and increased surface area all affect maneuver, firepower, and intelligence gathering.

2. Structures can degrade situational awareness at the tactical and
   operational levels of war.

3. The elements of infrastructure sustaining a city can be used as a
   tool of warfare, in both the physical and information realms.
   These same elements are necessary for residents' livelihood and
   should be left intact if feasible.

The operational and analytic dilemmas posed by urban construction
have been studied by U.S. and other nations' analysts. The material
on structural analysis in this work therefore seeks only to provide a
modest review of these efforts. Each of the problems associated with
urban terrain analysis will be discussed in terms of the three remaining major dilemmas of urban areas as introduced in Chapter Three:
underlying terrain, buildings, and infrastructure.

Analysis of an Urban Area's Underlying Terrain[13]

It has not gone unnoticed that a city's underlying terrain can play an
integral role in the success or failure of an urban operation. Consider
Mamaev Hill in Stalingrad and Nam San in Seoul. Both terrains provide excellent observation, fields of fire, and communications points
today, just as they did in 1942 and 1950 respectively. All officers are
taught the significance of understanding natural topography as part
of the operational planning process. Although the construction of
urban areas might overshadow the significance of the ground on
which the city stands, the underlying terrain should be understood
from the physical, historical, natural resource, and cultural perspec-

_____

[13]For an excellent overview of the type of considerations that should be made when
assessing the features of an urban area's underlying terrain, see MCIA-1540-002-95,
Generic Information Requirements Handbook, Quantico, VA: Marine Corps
Intelligence Activity, 1995.

tives if a unit is to understand and shape its operating environment in a full-dimensional effort, regardless of the type of operation undertaken.[14]

Mitrovica in Kosovo is an illustrative example of how a city's terrain affects all aspects of an operation. As shown in Figure 5.7, the Ibar River creates a natural line of communication (LOC) through the middle of the city. This LOC could be critical from a logistics standpoint, as a means of sustaining the force (as the Perfume River was in Hue City). The river is also an obstacle that bisects the built-up area. This bisection also creates a natural boundary between the two resident ethnic groups, Albanians and Serbs. The separation became significant at both the strategic and tactical levels in the 1999 deployments to Kosovo. U.S. forces had to ensure that the Orthodox Church located south of the Ibar was accessible to Serbs residing in the north. NATO peacekeepers built a footbridge across the river that allowed reliable, safe passage. The natural feature separating the two groups assisted the NATO troops in maintaining stability in the region. The bridge helped the soldiers focus their limited assets.

Analysis of an Urban Area's Construction

> To me it was a civil war; only it wasn't just the North against the South. It was North against South, East against West, Northeast against Southwest, Southeast against Northwest, and we were in the middle of it all. There were just too many different sides. If we picked one, we had four others against us.
>
> Thomas L. Friedman
> *From Beirut to Jerusalem*

Appendix G (IPB for MOUT) of FM 34-130/MCRP 2-12A (Coordinating Draft), FM 5-33, and Richard Ellefson's *Urban Terrain Zone Characteristics* describe similar methodologies for the analysis of a city's structural components. Each suggests that an evaluation of urban terrain should first consider the broad conditions that influence a city's layout and progressively provide more specific informa-

---

[14]For a discussion of the relevance of mapping products in all types of operations, see Richard Johnson, *Learning Unfamiliar Ground: Terrain Knowledge for Contingency Operations,* Carlisle Barracks, PA: U.S. Army War College, 1992.

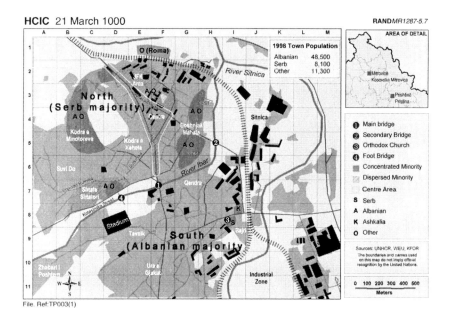

Figure 5.7—How Underlying Terrain Affects Urban Operations: Mitrovica

tion. For instance, Ellefson suggests that cities often follow the same developmental sequence—spreading from central core outward. As a result, the structural characteristics of whole sectors of the city can be hypothesized. Ellefson suggests that buildings within a central city core will tend to have more floors than buildings on the periphery. This is the result of property within the central core becoming more expensive as the city grows. This type of analysis assists in determining how buildings in a given section of the built-up area might influence force maneuver, survivability, and weapons' effects.

Similarly, FM 5-33, FM 90-10-1, FM 90-10, and FM 34-130 and its upcoming appendix on IPB for MOUT clearly define ways in which the analyst can categorize buildings based on outward appearance. For example, several of these manuals include descriptions of framed construction versus block construction or of the way a building's outward appearance might give clues to its interior configuration.

The designation of certain areas as types of zones based on construction materials, function, or building layout can help the analyst describe what the individual soldier can expect in a particular part of an urban area. For instance, in an industrial area the soldier can expect fewer intersections, thicker interior walls, and fewer windows but greater opportunities for vehicle concealment or materials storage. These combined characteristics work to limit the density of potential enemy firing positions while increasing the likelihood of heavy weapons that can better navigate the wider streets.

Presented in Table 5.4 are a few of the many IPB products have been developed to support urban terrain analysis. They are included here as a sampling of the myriad of ways the U.S. Army can evaluate the terrain characteristics of an urban area. As in the previous section of this chapter, products believed to be introduced for the first time are indicated as such. Unless otherwise indicated, the products described here are believed to be already in use by the armed services.

Situational awareness (SA) for the soldier on the street is necessary for any kind of operation. Available maps may not readily provide knowledge of all relevant street conditions, however. Maps may be too small in scale or fail to represent individual structures, underground passageways, or other features. Units from different services or even within a single service may possess different maps with possibly incompatible coordinate systems. As a result, it is suggested that every effort be made to ensure that the soldier on the street be given as much information as possible about the unique features of a city. Products that may assist in providing greater SA to the soldier and commander are listed in Table 5.5. Products in this table are already in use in the Army; those we believe to be new to the analytic toolset are indicated with the "Newly Introduced" label.

Table 5.4

Terrain Analysis Products

Terrain classification overlay

This overlay depicts the different terrain zones apparent in an urban area. Different types of terrain are indicated using hatch marks or other indicators on a map or aerial photograph. Zone types may be defined as close, orderly block, or dense random construction as in both FM 34-130 and FM 90-10, or by any other designated characteristics required by the mission, such as zones of threat occupation or zones divided by the types of predicted weapons effects.

Overlay of buildings and structures that are above a specific height

This product will provide information for the communications and air elements units. Another version could provide information on the presence and depth of basements.

Locations and conditions of shantytowns description and overlay

Shantytowns can be locations with notable food shortages and where disease and pollution are most prevalent. Shantytowns may lack public utility infrastructure (e.g., plumbing and electricity). Buildings are often made from miscellaneous materials, and there is no consistent pattern of streets or corridors, complicating military operations.

Mass assembly points overlay

This product is different from the congregation area overlay introduced as a demographic analysis product. The mass assembly points overlay should depict the number and types of locations (schools, churches, parks) that could be used to gather (for protection, feeding, or other purpose) large numbers of people in the event of disaster or emergency.

Road sustainability overlay

This overlay provides mobility information to assist planners and operators in determining what equipment can move along the city's mobility corridors. Pertinent data would include street widths, their load capacity, sharp turns, sniper positions, and overhanging obstacles.[a]

Table 5.4—continued

Unoccupied locations or buildings overlay (Newly Introduced)

Unoccupied locations or buildings can be used as shelter for troops or to demonstrate firepower if necessary. The latter utility was demonstrated in Kosovo when a tank round was shot into an unoccupied building in order to quell an increasingly worrisome civil disturbance.

Street widths with basement and upper floor dead space identification (Newly Introduced)

Determining street widths in terms of major weapon systems helps identify which formations or routes are most advisable for an area. A street wide enough to allow two Abrams tanks to advance side by side enables the vehicles to better cover upper floors on opposite sides of the street, thereby providing security for each other. Noting buildings that exceed the depression or elevation capabilities of a vehicle denote areas of notable concern and potential enemy ambush positions. Routes with such "dead spaces" may require convoys with additional or alternative systems able to eliminate this vulnerability.

Dead space tracking overlay for air operations (Newly Introduced)[b]

The dead space tracking overlay reflects areas around buildings or other urban features that preclude air defense engagements of rotary-wing aircraft, or areas where engagement opportunities are limited. Aviation units can plot routes that maximize the use of such dead space to minimize their vulnerability to air defense weapons available to the adversary. Similarly, friendly force air defense units should coordinate with maneuver units to cover such areas with systems that compensate for anti-air capabilities.

Sniper position identification overlay

This overlay pinpoints potential sniper positions along each relevant avenue of approach based on the best possible locations given line of sight, elevation, exposure, and other pertinent considerations.

[a]Other relevant data to be considered are included in MCIA-1540-002-95, *Generic Information Requirements Handbook,* Quantico, VA: Marine Corps Intelligence Activity, 1995, especially chapters 12 and 13.

[b]This product is introduced and discussed in Sean J.A. Edwards, *Freeing Mercury's Wings: Improving Tactical Communications in Cities,* Santa Monica, CA: RAND, MR-1316-A, 2001.

Table 5.5

Situational Awareness Products

Landmark overlay (Newly Introduced)

This overlay depicts notable features. Landmarks may be more helpful (and less mutable) than street signs, providing the soldier with things to look for to help orient him. Ideally, a landmark is recognizable even if demolished.

Street name overlay

This product provides easy-to-remember names for streets. Streets are given more easily remembered names in lieu of actual designations. Soldiers in Mogadishu used this practice, calling a major thoroughfare "Dead Cow Road" rather than "Hawlwadig Road."

Deployment descriptions for inter-story operations

These devices are to assist in the building-clearing tactics used by small units. Used with the labeling techniques provided by Ellefson and the upcoming IPB for MOUT appendix to FM 34-130, the floors of a building should be marked according to which unit would be deployed to each. Rules of communication between floors should also be included. For example, based on the layout of a multistory building, one squad of a platoon can be tasked to clear alternate floors, while another squad is tasked to clear and ready the rest for use as a reconnaissance base. Communication guidelines between squads should be established, including channel selection (if radio is used), activity descriptors, when communication is acceptable, and other C2 procedures.

Moving obstacles overlay (Newly Introduced)

This product will depict the most likely locations of rubble, noncombatants, and unarmed combatants. It will give the soldier an idea of the relative chaos associated with employing his weapon in different sectors of the city. For instance, it can be used to depict how and where a city's population gathers and the locations of the LOCs that the population uses to get to these gathering places. It can also include areas where rubble or other material can be used to alter LOCs that might be used by the friendly unit.

Analysis of an Urban Area's Infrastructure

As discussed previously, a city's infrastructure might be essential to fulfilling the logistical needs of a force or the city's population. The infrastructure can also be a tool of physical or information warfare. Identifying which structures are most critical is a first step toward ensuring that the interests of military and civilian users are suitably met. Electrical, sewage, and water systems, should be identified as critical infrastructure. Other infrastructure, such as media outlets and transmission locations, as well as financial institutions, should also be included in this analysis. Locations of civil authority centers such as fire and police stations, seats of government, and the like should also be identified. When identifying these important nodes of urban sustainability, the analyst should seek to incorporate all infrastructure that could potentially affect missions, both those already assigned and those likely to be assigned in the future.

Additional IPB products that can assist in urban infrastructure analysis appear in Table 5.6. These products, like the rest in this chapter, are based on what is already available to the command staff, unless otherwise noted with the "Newly Introduced" label. There are many more products that are available or can be easily produced using the list of questions provided by the USMC *GIRH*. Additionally, as with the other products presented, each can be used independently or together, depending on the needs of the commander and his mission.

URBAN WEATHER ANALYSIS

Along with typical weather patterns, cities have their own microclimates that can affect operations. Dust, smog, wind channeling, night illumination, and sun reflection off buildings are all "weather conditions" that could alter a unit's traditional TTPs. These conditions are often transitory or initiated by friendly force actions. Dust plumes from helicopters is one example. There are certain conditions related to natural occurrences that, although not necessarily weather-related, fit most logically into the weather analysis category. For instance, certain cities, or parts of a city, may have a particular odor that can distract the soldier. A product used to map the path this odor generally follows might better prepare the soldier for the

Table 5.6

Products Used to Identify and Assess Critical Infrastructure

"Untouchable" terrain overlay

"Untouchable" terrain encompasses areas that should not be destroyed, attacked, or occupied, or that have other use restrictions based on international treaties, ROE, and common sense—such as schools, hospitals, areas with large amounts of phone and/or electrical wiring, and buildings with many stories.

Media facilities overlay

This includes locations of transmission stations, antennas, newspaper production sites, and television and radio stations. The overlay can be produced by using a map, aerial photography or graphic design that is appropriately marked with a numbering or color-coded system that indicates the type of asset as well as its specific attributes.

Transportation facilities overlay

This overlay indicates rail hubs, major bus connection sites, subway lines, freeways, major thoroughfares, and intersections that are significant to the operation.

Resource sites overlay

This overlay can depict locations where resources or supplies can be obtained, such as building material locations, car lots, and appliance warehouses. The Marine Corps *GIRH* has a chapter devoted to petroleum and natural gas processing plants that provides a very useful guide to evaluating the types of resources and infrastructure that are used to support the critical resource needs of a population.

Critical infrastructure overlay

Electricity generation plants, pumping stations, water purification plants, sewage treatment plants, and anything that if harmed can affect the living conditions of the population should be depicted. The Marine Corps *GIRH* includes in this analysis the size and construction of hydroelectric dams.[a]

Subterranean infrastructure overlay

This overlay can indicate underground railways, sewer systems, electrical wiring, or any other underground feature of significance for the operation.

Table 5.6—continued

Dangerous facilities overlay

Structures with known chemical, biological, or incendiary features, such as pharmaceutical plants, oil refineries, or fertilizer plants, should be identified. The Marine Corps *GIRH* also addresses ammunition storage facilities (chapter 26).

[a]MCIA-1540-002-95, *Generic Information Requirements Handbook,* Quantico, VA: Marine Corps Intelligence Activity, 1995, chapter 23.

potential distraction. This same logic can be used to track how hazardous gases can disperse in the atmosphere, or how a fire might spread. Therefore, in addition to the weather products that are traditionally created for all types of operations, some that are specifically adapted to accommodate urban weather effects must also be constructed. Considerations that might be included in urban weather analysis are:

- Dust storms created by helicopter rotor blades kicking up the dirt from the street, inhibiting troop movement and deployment.

- Extreme heat from being confined to small places or from the sun reflecting off asphalt may also hamper troop effectiveness.

- The city's effect on night operations is also significant. Traditionally, U.S. forces "own the night." The extra luminescence provided by the ambient light of the city may neutralize this superiority. In addition, residents of the city are familiar with its layout and can maneuver easily in darkness. It is, therefore, necessary to consider this effect when conducting the overall weather analysis for the city.

- Smog inversion layers are common over cities. An inversion layer may trap dust, smoke, and chemicals in the air that can be detrimental to the health of soldiers. If the conditions are severe enough, protective gas masks may be needed during some types of operations. Weather analysis products for urban IPB are similar to those for traditional IPB but should include these peculiarities.

SUMMARY OF IPB STEP TWO FOR URBAN OPERATIONS

Compared to actions conducted on open terrain, operations in urban areas require the intelligence analyst to assess the effects of more factors. Populations, buildings, and infrastructure must all be assessed in order to ensure a unit's success. Elements of the population must be identified based on several demographic criteria, and then they must be understood using the cultural intelligence tools provided. With this information, the unit will not only be assisted in deploying its maneuver battlefield operating systems (BOS), the CA, PA, and PSYOP components can also be more effectively deployed.

Terrain analysis for an urban area must include how the three-dimensional nature of the terrain and the area's construction types affect all sections of a unit. Infrastructure must be included in the analysis because of its life-sustaining ability and its relevance as a tool of both physical and information warfare.

Urban weather is unique. A city may have its own microclimate that could affect and be affected by the presence of the unit. Considering how the unit can use the microclimate to its advantage and how it will affect the force might be challenging due to the transitory nature of some weather conditions.

Chapter Six

IPB FOR URBAN OPERATIONS STEP THREE: IDENTIFY AND EVALUATE THREATS AND RELEVANT INFLUENCES

However absorbed a commander may be in the elaboration of his own thoughts, it is sometimes necessary to take the enemy into account.

Winston Churchill

The fundamental responsibility of intelligence is to provide decision makers at all levels of command the fullest possible understanding of the adversary. This understanding includes a sophisticated knowledge of the adversary's goals, objectives, strategy, intentions, capabilities, methods of operation, vulnerabilities and sense of value and loss.

Joint Publication 2-0
Joint Intelligence Support to Military Operations

[F]ew populations are ever exclusively hostile, or truly indifferent, or unreservedly welcoming. Man's complexity is richer than any architectural detail. It is, finally, the people, armed and dangerous, watching for exploitable opportunities, or begging to be protected, who will determine the success or failure of the intervention.

Ralph Peters
"The Human Terrain of Urban Operations"

Throughout military history, misunderstanding or underestimating the capabilities of an adversary has proved disastrous. Pearl Harbor, Vietnam, and Mogadishu all serve as reminders that a seemingly invincible U.S. force can be surprised and overcome. Several factors contributed to the U.S. defeats in each of these instances. Unquestionably, one of those factors was a lack of adequate information about the threat.

One of the conditions that sets Mogadishu apart from the other two examples is that units deployed in Somalia were overwhelmed by an opposition composed, in part, of those whom the soldiers were originally deployed to assist. The fact that the Somalis' posture changed from "neutral" or "friendly" to "enemy" during the operation raises several questions. One relevant to this work is: Could IPB (threat evaluation specifically) have predicted this shift and helped coalition decisionmakers avoid it? Although this question may be impossible to answer, we postulate that people's actions and allegiances change the threat picture during an operation. Further, we think that the resultant changes can be identified, evaluated, and even manipulated in the service of mission accomplishment.

It is important to first understand why urban operations like those in Mogadishu, in which civilians on the battlefield are commonplace, create difficulties for traditional threat evaluation. After a brief discussion of this complicating element, we investigate the urban-specific implications of threat definition and introduce a new approach for identifying and evaluating threats and those influences not sufficiently analyzed during steps one and two.

CURRENT DILEMMAS OF THREAT EVALUATION FOR URBAN OPERATIONS

Why Urban Areas Pose Dilemmas for Traditional Threat Evaluation

The people, buildings, and infrastructure in an urban area inhibit straightforward threat evaluation by obscuring both threat identity and threat capabilities, and by introducing myriad other influences that may negatively, positively, or benignly influence friendly force operations. There is also a multitude of such possible threats and influences. A variety of active, passive, and latent population elements can potentially influence friendly and enemy (if present) force operations in any type of urban mission. Being able to assess the *level of threat* or *opportunity* each element imposes is fundamental to mission success. The greater density and multiple interrelationships of individuals found in built-up areas increase the complexity of categorization. Nevertheless, for the purposes of planning, force protection, and conducting operations it is necessary to have a way to place each group on a continuum that effectively depicts "threatening" and "nonthreatening" sectors of the population.

The effort is not a one-time undertaking. The categorization will require constant review. Groups and individuals can be cajoled, forced, or co-opted into providing or withholding services to either the friendly or opposing force. People act opportunistically, ready to shift alliances as perceived advantages arise. Looking after their own interests, some will actively seek to maximize profit rather than retain one or another side's goodwill. The posture of groups, and members within groups, should therefore be considered variable.

Even seemingly passive and law-abiding members of a populace may conduct themselves in unexpected ways given the right conditions. During the Los Angeles riots of 1992, for example, looting and destruction of property was perpetrated by otherwise law-abiding citizens. The *opportunistic* nature of conditions is one cause of this phenomenon. Instability, the breakdown of legal authority, and the chance to immerse oneself in the protective environment of a crowd are all conditions that stimulate such behavior. All are conditions frequently apparent during urban operations.

Population groups or individuals can *unwittingly interfere* with operations and thereby increase friendly force exposure. Refugee flows and members of the media have already been used as examples of how people can impede friendly force actions by merely doing what is necessary for their own well-being.

Groups or individuals can also be *manipulated* by either the friendly or opposing force, by other parties, or by events themselves. Such manipulation may be with or without the knowledge of the subjects influenced. A captured opponent asked to provide HUMINT is an example of the former circumstance; the use of PSYOP or CA to influence the activity of a population exemplifies the latter.

These and other dilemmas require modification of IPB traditional step three, *evaluate the threat*. The familiar cookbook-type formula that allows the intelligence officer to plot the personnel, materiel, and tactics of a known enemy is no longer sufficient. Step three of IPB for urban operations must first *identify* the elements, human and otherwise, that can *harm, interfere with, or otherwise significantly influence* friendly force activities. Once identified, the most mission-significant elements can be prioritized for fuller evaluation. Others can be handled as time allows.

Thus, step three of IPB for urban operations includes the following:

- An *identification* phase in which all population groups and sub-groups are arrayed along a continuum denoting their interests relative to the friendly force (or to each other). Entities that can threaten, interfere with, or otherwise significantly influence operations are noted for further evaluation.

- A *prioritization* of these entities based on the degree to which they can impact mission accomplishment.

- *Evaluation* that includes tactics, techniques, and procedures perhaps not generally encountered in other environments.

The next subsection considers current doctrinal shortfalls with respect to threat evaluation. It is hoped that this discussion will assist in understanding the proposed new approaches that follow. Thereafter, the analysis turns to ways to overcome the aforementioned dilemmas posed by the presence of many population groups within urban areas.

Doctrinal Dilemmas of Threat Evaluation

There is no doctrinal definition of "threat."[1]   Current MOOTW instructional materials available from United States Army Intelligence Center and Fort Huachuca (USAIC & FH), however, describe the threat in stability and support operation (SASO) scenarios as "anything that threatens mission accomplishment." When deployed as part of a combat operation against a clear adversary, the direct military threat is known and evaluation can proceed as dictated by the three-step process outlined in FM 34-130/MCRP 2-12A:

---

[1]As identified in JP 2-01, *Joint Intelligence Support to Military Operations,* FM 100-5, *Operations,* FM 101-5-1, *Operational Terms and Graphics,* and FM 34-130/MCRP 2-12A, *Intelligence Preparation of the Battlefield.*

1. Identify the threat.

2. Update or create threat models.

3. Identify threat capabilities.

For noncombat operations, and for combat in urban areas where noncombatants dwell, the lack of a clear definition poses several analytic problems for the S2/G2/J2:

1. The lack of a clear doctrinal definition allows for ambiguous implementation of threat evaluation. Analysts, not knowing what to assess, might assess the wrong element, too many elements, or an insufficient number of elements.

2. The MOOTW definition presupposes that a threat must exist, leading to an "us-versus-them" mentality that might seek to find a threat when one does not exist.

3. Related to point 2 above, the analyst may overlook the possibility that some elements of the environment can assist in accomplishing the mission as he pursues identification of one or more "threats."

FM 34-7 (Initial Draft), *IEW for Stability Operations and Support Operations,* begins to alleviate some of these dilemmas by introducing additional threat evaluation components. According to the manual, threat analysis should include information from five categories: the battlefield environment (terrain, hydrology, weather), threat organizational structure, friendly force organizational structure, population, and physical objects. The information used to fill the requirements relevant to each of these categories, combined with traditional threat-modeling procedures (composition, disposition, strength, personalities), helps to determine what type of threat or other influence is apparent during each type of mission.

FM 34-7 also advises that, at the very least, intelligence analysts should determine the relative disposition of most of the population subgroups within the AO; sectors of the population should be labeled "neutral," "friendly," or "enemy" depending on which side, if any, each group seems to favor (doctrinally this concept is as depicted in Figure 6.1). This step is intended to mitigate situational uncertainty

RAND*MR1287-6.1*

Enemy—Neutral—Friendly

Figure 6.1—Doctrinal Categories for Assessing the Population

by providing an idea of the level of support or resistance a friendly unit might encounter within designated areas.

The analytic procedures proposed in FM 34-7—considering additional components of the AO as possible threats and assessing the relative loyalty of extant population groups—begin to demonstrate that threat evaluation is not a straightforward assessment of the capabilities of a known, armed adversary. Rather, the diverse populations and "nonmilitary" elements that are apparent in any operational area require consideration during threat assessment, because of their abilities to affect operations. But labeling all these elements within the three categories of "neutral," "friendly," or "enemy" does not remove all of the analytic pitfalls described earlier. For instance, using the three categories does not elementally alter the essentially bipolar perspective of the operational environment; the labels lack the necessary degree of nuance. An alternative approach for tackling this shortfall is proposed in the next section.

IDENTIFYING THREATS AND RELEVANT INFLUENCES: THE CONTINUUM OF RELATIVE INTEREST

> [S]ometimes I don't know what we are doing. During the day, the people in Gudermes smile at us and bring us goodies. But at night, they are out there shooting at us. I don't know whom we are protecting from whom.
>
> Michael Gordon
> "In Occupied Chechnya, Order Comes Without Allegiance"

Interestingly, whether or not an entity is a friend or enemy changes quickly. To gain an appreciation of the multiplicity of threats, MI professionals must first recognize, then understand, the tapestry of existing relationships among them.

> LTG Claudia Kennedy

Noncombatants and refugees without hostile intent can still overwhelm the force of an advancing platoon. The logistics needed to provide for and contain an urban population in the millions can be overwhelming. There may be enemy military troops, criminal gangs, vigilantes, paramilitary factions within militaries, and factions within those factions hiding within the waves of the displaced. The enemy knows that it will be impossible to tell friend from foe from disinterested.

Marine Corps Intelligence Activity
The Urban Century: Developing World Urban Trends and Possible Factors Affecting Military Operations

As discussed in the previous chapter, there are population groups, subgroups, and individuals present in an urban area that have the capability to exploit a friendly vulnerability without the slightest intent to do so. It is merely by following the innate mechanisms of self-interest that these elements might undermine friendly activities. Given the imprecise nature of current doctrine—having to label actors as "friendly," "neutral," or "enemy"—it is difficult to determine how to categorize these elements. Should they be considered aligned with the enemy because they are degrading the success of the mission (whether deliberately or inadvertently)? Should these elements be considered neutral if their troublesome actions are other than deliberate? Putting a group within either one of these categories without assessing its full potential to influence mission accomplishment can impede mission success.

An alternative method of labeling the level of threat, utility, and manipulability a population element poses relative to a friendly force is warranted. The "continuum of relative interests" (newly introduced by the authors in this report), discussed below, allows the analyst to array each element of a population along a continuum that indicates level of threat posed and utility offered based on the group's unique characteristics. The continuum helps to depict each element's susceptibility to manipulation and assists the friendly force analyst in visualizing how these elements, if manipulated, might shift from one part of the continuum to another—a feature that will be of considerable assistance during course-of-action (COA) development and war gaming. Further, the continuum assists the user in determining force protection needs, identifying antipathies between groups, and measuring a group's level of required support (e.g., during a mission involving the supply of food, water, or other essentials).

Thus the objectives sought in applying and using the continuum are

1. To determine a given element's potential utility in meeting mission demands.

2. To determine an element's potential for manipulation.

3. To provide a basis for detecting and monitoring shifts in relevant relationships.

The terms used to characterize each of the population elements are defined below. A consideration of how elements of a population might be evaluated using these terms follows thereafter. The discussion of the *continuum of relative interests* concludes with a demonstration of how to use it as a dynamic tool of ongoing threat assessment and operation management. It is important to note that the term "relative" is a notable facet of the continuum's value; where a given group or element appears on the continuum may differ depending on the perspective from which it is viewed. For example, the United States might have viewed a given Mogadishu clan as "adversary," whereas the Italians, with their colonial background in the region, could have considered it "neutral" or even "friendly."

A New Definition of Threat

Three components are inherent in all doctrinal and anecdotal discussions of a threat:

*   Threats possess the capability to inflict harm

*   Threats have the intention to inflict harm

*   There exists a friendly vulnerability to harm

We propose that a "threat" does not exist if any of these components is missing. We do not assume, however, that the friendly force is not impervious to peril. There are likely to be friendly vulnerabilities that are unknown to the friendly force. Equally likely is the fact that a group may have hidden interests or intentions to threaten the friendly force, or hidden capabilities to do harm to the friendly unit.

What we propose here is not a strict definition. This new definition of threat is meant to parse the different components of what appears to constitute a threat, in order to thoroughly analyze each population group within the operational area. Based on the evaluation of each component, a determination can be made of the most threatening elements facing the friendly force. Using the three components of threat listed above, we propose our own definition of "adversary" to ground our discussion of how to categorize population groups along the *continuum of relative interests*. For the purposes of this study, we define adversary as follows:

> An adversary has some current *capability* and *intention* to nega-tively influence mission accomplishment by exploiting a friendly *vulnerability*.

Joint Publication 1-02, *Department of Defense Dictionary of Military and Associated Terms*, defines each of the highlighted components of the above definition.

Capability*:* The ability to execute a specified course of action (a capability may or may not be accompanied by an intention).[2]

Intention*:* An aim or design (as distinct from capability) to exe-cute a specified course of action.[3]

Vulnerability*:* 1. The susceptibility of a nation or military force to any action by any means through which its war potential or combat effectiveness may be reduced or his will to fight dimin-ished. 2. The characteristics of a system which cause it to suffer a definite degradation (incapability to perform the designated mission) as a result of having been subjected to a certain level of effects in an unnatural (manmade) hostile environment.[4]

An additional key component to this discussion is the difference be-tween interest and intention.

---

[2]JP 1-02, *Department of Defense Dictionary of Military and Associated Terms,* Washington, D.C.: Office of the Joint Chiefs of Staff, 1994, p. 67.

[3]Ibid., p. 225.

[4]Ibid., p. 475.

Interest: The underlying motivation for the pursuit of an activity. For example, one has an interest in eating to survive.[5]

Intention: The mode (doctrinally, the aim or design) chosen to fulfill the corresponding interest: one may intend to fulfill the interest of eating by buying food, picking it from a tree, stealing it, or trading something for it.

The difference between interest and intent is important to keep in mind when considering how to influence different elements of a population (and how to do so if manipulation is desirable). Interests influence intentions. The previously cited example of the U.S. Navy's use of the Mafia in New York during World War II helps to illustrate the difference between interest and intent. Making money and operating without law enforcement investigations were among Mafia interests. There were manifold ways the Mafia could have intended to pursue these interests (e.g., remaining hidden from the law, killing investigators, or cooperating with authorities). Interestingly, the Mafia was also interested in assisting the U.S. war effort. At the time, it had control over New York harbor operations. This control gave the organization the capability to pursue its more notorious endeavors. It also gave it the capability to assist the U.S. Navy in maintaining port security. This duality created a condition in which a seemingly threatening group, one that would doctrinally be considered "enemy," could also be considered "friendly" because of its ability to assist in the accomplishment of a friendly force mission. The U.S. Navy was able to use the patriotic position of the Mafia, along with other methods of suasion and coercion, to manipulate the Mafia's capability. The Navy effectively steered the organization's intent to one of cooperation with authorities rather than hiding from or interfering with the law.[6]

Using the above definitions as criteria for assessing the nature and utility of each population element, the authors propose that the members of the command and intelligence staffs can place each group identified in IPB step two on the *continuum of relative interests*

---

[5]*Merriam Webster's Collegiate Dictionary, Tenth Edition,* Springfield, MA: 1998.

[6]Carlo D'este, *Bitter Victory: The Battle for Sicily 1943,* Glasgow: William Collins Sons and Co. Ltd, 1988.

(shown in Figure 6.2) using the following categories as guides. Definitions are the authors':

Adversary: A population element with the capability, interest, and intent to exploit a friendly vulnerability.

Obstacle: A population element with an active capability to exploit a friendly vulnerability. Current interests may or may not be compatible with friendly force goals, but there is no intention to interfere with friendly force activities.

Neutral: A population element whose interests do not conflict with either the friendly or the adversarial force. Capability to affect the friendly force mission may exist, but it is currently inert.

Accomplice: A population element with the capability to capitalize on a friendly or adversary vulnerability whose intentions are compatible with friendly force objectives.

Ally: A population element whose interest and intent is to assist in accomplishing friendly force objectives.

It is important to understand that the labels are meant as guides only. Population groups and subgroups do not necessarily fit into one category rather than another. Each group can be off-center in a particular category; it can have components in two or more categories simultaneously; or it can shift among categories during an operation. The latter two conditions are apparent in the Mafia example described above. Similarly, a given group may have individuals within it that have relative interests that differ from those of the entire group or its major subgroups.

RAND*MR1287-6.2*

Adversary—Obstacle—Neutral—Accomplice—Ally

Figure 6.2—The Continuum of Relative Interests

The most critical population sectors will frequently be those lying in the middle of the spectrum, within or near the obstacle, neutral, and accomplice categories. These groups would constitute "the important segment" as described by Lieutenant General Vijay Madan of the Indian Army, who defines such elements as the "uncommitted segment without any interest in the conflict [or other type of operation], but the element which has yet to make up its mind."[7] The significance of the important segment cannot be overstated. What is inherent in the definition is that the uncommitted population might have the capability to influence either the friendly or adversary (if applicable) mission, but it does not currently have the intention to act decisively one way or another. If the interests of the uncommitted segment can be understood by the friendly force, there is an opportunity to shape the intentions of this segment (or a relevant part of it) to assist in accomplishing the friendly mission.

An example helps to further clarify terms and begins to demonstrate the utility of a spectrum with the nuances found on the *continuum of relative interests*.[8] The economic (or some other) elite of a city may possess more power than the central state government. This small group could isolate itself physically and socially from sprawling poor communities while continuing to wield enormous power over the country's political future. These wealthy may have alliances with criminal organizations. They might also be likely to act as patrons for selected individuals within the government. The elite group could be defined in several ways were an insurgency to threaten the urban area it inhabits. This group clearly has the monetary capability and political influence to help either the ruling government or an insurgent group. The insurgents could co-opt the criminal organizations of the city to elicit funding (through intimidation) from the elites— making the elite group an accomplice to the insurgent cause. Conversely, the ruling government might procure assistance from the elites by promising continued maintenance of the social status quo despite popular pressures for alternatives. The categories into which

---

[7]Lieutenant General Vijay Madan, "Population Terrain: The Neglected Factor of Counter-Insurgency Operations," *Indian Defense Review,* April–June 1997, Vol. 12, No. 2, p. 8.

[8]Example adapted from Marine Corps Intelligence Activity, *The Urban Century: Developing World Urban Trends and Possible Factors Affecting Military Operations,* MCIA-1586-003-9, Quantico, VA: U.S. Marine Corps, 1997.

the elites fall will ultimately depend on their individual and collective interests—do the elites have a greater interest in survival or in power? Are the two mutually exclusive? Is there something that can prevent them from getting either? The Los Angeles riots of 1992 provide a real-world example of how population groups can shift their relative positions due to changing conditions within the operational area. Several gangs exist in the Los Angeles area. Usually, these gangs are adversarial to one another. During the riots, however, several of the rival gangs formed a "united front" against what was seen as a larger obstacle to their own interests: law enforcement. As a result, the adversarial gangs became one another's accomplices during that time.

The foregoing examples demonstrate that population groups, and the relationships among them, are not static. Group intentions and relationships change as conditions and other relevant relationships change. To understand how this can happen, and how these changing conditions can be used, manipulated, or even ignored while accomplishing the friendly mission, questions on each group's interests, intentions, and capabilities need to be asked. Answers to these questions will help to array the relevant population groups (identified as part of IPB step two) along the *continuum of relative interests,* a tool that aids in COA development, which includes predicting the higher-order effects of any activity within the operational area. The following discussion provides some suggestions on how to analyze each population group as well as how to assess the vulnerabilities of the friendly force.

Capability assessment. The first step in categorizing a population element and identifying its role(s) as a threat or influence is to conduct a cursory evaluation of each element's capabilities. The matrix in Figure 6.3 shows how this evaluation can be undertaken for each relevant group. Several of these matrices will be necessary to evaluate all the resident elements of the AO and AOI. This matrix is presented as a guide only and can be modified to suit the commander and his mission. Additionally, this matrix is adaptable to the idea that particular capabilities can be considered named areas of interest, target areas of interest, high-value targets, or high-payoff targets. Although these labels are currently given only to specific points or assets in the physical realm, according to doctrine, it is proposed that these or similar labels can also be used for the often less tangible points presented here.

The categories in the above capabilities matrix are not exhaustive; more can be added when necessary or desired. In addition, column and row headings should change to appropriately fit particular operational requirements. The information being captured by this matrix is intended to show the following:

- **The inherent capabilities of each population group that could be used to hinder or assist U.S. forces, intentionally or unintentionally.** These capabilities should be considered objectively. Assets should not be attributed with either malice or friendly intent at this point.

- **Determination of the nature of the relationships between population elements identified in urban IPB step two.** The relationships identified in urban IPB step two are critical components of threat identification. Relationships between each relevant group should be characterized by which population elements interact, why they interact, and the temperament of the interaction. In this way, it is possible to identify likely flash points or points of collusion between two population elements.

- **Descriptions of population element interdependencies.** Possible points of exploitation can be highlighted by identifying dependencies between elements. These potential critical points can be the source of future contention or used to mollify creeping animosity.

When completing the matrix, the intelligence analyst can also begin to identify intelligence requirements (IR), high-value targets (HVT), high-payoff targets (HPT), and named areas of interest (NAI) that are not otherwise easily mapped. For instance, any cell of the matrix that does not have sufficient information might be considered an IR; the urgency associated with completing the cell will help establish its priority (e.g., should the information be a PIR?). The type of information required to fill the cell will determine its type (is the information a FFIR, PIR, or EEFI?).[9] HVT can be identified as those assets

---

[9]See Chapter Two for definition of these intelligence requirements.

| Combat Capabilities | | | | |
	Composition	Primary Characteristics	Availability	Location	Consequences
Weapons	Number and type of weapons. (This may be N/A if the group is not combative.)	Descriptions of weapons and weapons effects.	Are there enough for the entire group? How is resupply handled?	Where are they stored?	How will this capability affect friendly operations? Consider both positive and negative effects.
Equipment	What type of logistics capability exists? What types of transportation are used?	Descriptions of equipment and transportation means.	Are there enough for the entire group? How is resupply handled?	Same as above.	Same as above.
Personnel	Force strength.	Descriptions of weapons and weapons effects.	Are there enough for the entire group? How is resupply handled?	Where are they stationed?	Same as above.
Leadership	Who leads? What is the leadership structure? Is there a hierarchy or network?	How is leadership maintained (coercion, persuasion, loyalty)? Is the leadership strong or tenuous?	Is the presence of a leader necessary to the functioning of the group? How often is the leadership apparent? In what forum/format is the leadership seen?	Does the leadership have a single location?	What will happen to the population group and/or friendly unit under this leadership? What if the leadership is removed?
Tactics	Generic sense of tactics used. For unarmed combatants this may be a description of how they assist armed combatants.	Description of TTP.	How are tactics trained?	Where are certain tactics most prevalent?	How will this capability affect friendly operations? Consider both positive and negative effects.

Figure 6.3—Population Element Capabilities Assessment Matrix (Newly Introduced)

Information Operations Capabilities

	Composition	Primary Characteristics	Availability	Location	Consequences
Infrastructure	What type of mechanism for IO is owned? Radio station, TV, newspaper, graffiti, hand gestures, word of mouth?	Reach scope, target audience. Where does it get its functionality?	Is the mechanism used to relay the message reliable? What are its deficiencies? How often is IO used and in how many different ways?	Where is the source located? Where are the messages most displayed or heard?	How will this capability affect friendly operations? Consider both positive and negative effects.
Audience	Demographic of target audience and those actually receiving the message.	What are the capabilities of the audience? Does the message purport to fulfill any critical interest of the target audience?	How often is the audience within reach?	Where is the audience located? How are spatial gaps bridged?	What kind of effect can the audience have on the mission?
Message	What is the message? Who is the target audience and why are they targeted?	What are the cultural components of the message? Are they exclusive, or do they seek to incorporate a wide audience? Is the message culturally acceptable? Can the message be manipulated in any way? How?	How often is the message relayed?	Where is the message being seen or heard?	What if the message did not get out? What if it was misinterpreted by the audience?
Messenger	What individual or group is constructing the message?	Who is the intended audience? What is being sought by the transmitter of the message? Will the audience listen? Can the message be mitigated or countered?			What are the consequences of losing the messenger? Can the messenger be shaped to suit friendly force needs?

Figure 6.3—continued

Dependencies

	Composition	Primary Characteristics	Availability	Location	Consequences
Living needs (water, food, health care)	What is the need? Who fulfills the need?	How is the need fulfilled? Is it adequately fulfilled? Are there other sources that can fulfill the need? How disparate is the fulfilled need from what is expected? How disparate is it from the norm?	Is there sufficient supply? How often is the store resupplied?	Where is the source fulfilling the need located? Where are those in need?	What would happen if this need were not met? What kind of relationship could be forged in order to meet this need?
Human needs (water, power, disposal)	Same as above.	Same as above.	Same as above.	Same as above.	Same as above.
Cultural needs (religion, schools, government)	Same as above.	Same as above.	Same as above.	Same as above.	Same as above.
Economic	Same as above.	Same as above.	Same as above.	Same as above.	Same as above.
Protection	Who needs protection? Who is providing the protection?	Are the people being protected from a particular group? What is that group? Are they refugees or in their homes? Why do they need protection?	Is the unit able to provide this protection? Does the unit depend on another group to help protect?	Is protection based on locale of population? Does protection switch from one group to the next when location is different? Does the second protecting group have different SOP?	Same as above.

Figure 6.3—continued

Capabilities for Autonomous Operability

	Composition	Primary Characteristics	Availability	Location	Consequences
Living needs (water, food, health care)	How are they providing for themselves?	How is the need fulfilled? Is it adequately fulfilled? Are there other sources that can fulfill the need? How disparate is the fulfilled need from what is expected? How disparate is it from the norm?	Is it readily available? If not, what is the cause of the intermittent availability?	Where is the source fulfilling the need located? Where are those in need? How far must they travel?	What would happen if this need were not met? What kind of relationship could be forged in order to meet this need?
Human needs (water, power, disposal)	Same as above.	Same as above.	Same as above.	Same as above.	Same as above.
Cultural needs (religion, schools, government)	Same as above.	Same as above.	Same as above.	Same as above.	Same as above.
Economic	Same as above.	Same as above.	Same as above.	Same as above.	Same as above.
Protection	Who within the group provides protection?	How is the protection provided?	Is protection always available?	Is protection only provided in certain locales?	Same as above.

Figure 6.3—continued

Relationships With Other Elements

	Composition	Primary Characteristics	Availability	Location	Consequences
Element X	Who comprises the actors involved in the relationship?	Why are the two groups related? Does a dependency exist? Are they in conflict? What are the characteristics of interaction (mutually supportive? combative?) How do they communicate with each other? Can the relationship be manipulated? Is it a bond based on need/trust/history or convenience?	How often do the elements interact?	Where do elements interact directly? Are there any indirect connections?	How does this relationship affect the political and/or social balance of the operational area? How does the relationship affect the friendly unit's operations?
Element Y	Same as above.	Same as above.	Same as above.	Same as above.	Same as above.

Figure 6.3—continued

believed held by a certain group (as is traditionally done). Or, it can be identified as a relationship that becomes apparent as a result of mapping the dependencies and interconnections between groups. As discussed previously, the idea of assigning specifically defined doctrinal terms to relationships rather than tangible assets or events might not prove beneficial for all command staffs. The use of this proposed convention is offered for consideration only, and while it might prove useful for some staff members during some operations, it should not be seen as a fixed solution for all types of operations. These ideas might lead to an expansion of the definition of each of the labels, or create new doctrinal labels for the intended use. With this caveat in mind, we will proceed with the idea that the labels can be adapted for identifying critical relationships among elements of an urban operational area.

Depicting relationships and dependencies between groups in matrix form aids in focusing intelligence assets on the most critical relationships and might help in determining courses of action for each group in question. These items are often difficult to visualize using only traditional IPB products. Using the capabilities matrix depicted above, NAIs can be established that are not related to any specific location. These NAIs seek to pinpoint situations or exchanges that can be viewed as confirming or denying a nontraditional COA. For instance, NAIs can be meetings between two groups, the fulfillment of a basic need, or a change in the amount of communication between two population elements.

It is important to note that the capabilities list does not include value judgments. A specific combat capability, for instance, should not lead the analyst to conclude that this capability will be used against the friendly force. The capability should be viewed as a potential threat, obstacle, or asset. For example, the friendly force, if necessary, could use a group's weapons cache to serve its own needs. Additionally, the group itself, depending on its interests and intentions, might be co-opted by the friendly force to assist mission accomplishment.

Interests and intention assessment. Evaluating the interests and intentions of a group is a problematic component of the threat identification process. It is often difficult to understand population group motivations. However, five steps help in initially determining interests and intentions:

1. **Review the cultural intelligence derived in the second step of urban IPB.** Are there historical examples that might indicate intentions or predisposition? Does the historical record provide evidence on the means a group might employ to support its interests? Have there been changes in the urban environment (e.g., growth in economic influence by an opposing demographic group or an electoral victory of another faction's candidate) that might foretell changes in behavior from the historical norm?

2. **Study ongoing and past reactions to the operation itself.** How are population elements responding to events? Are there trends? Are there telltale signs of conditions that might elicit a certain type of response?

3. **Follow local and international news—be cognizant of the facts, the perceptions, and the message.** Many times the interests or intentions of a population element might be directly reported. If not, they can sometimes be inferred by the nature of the reporting. However, too great a reliance on this type of indicator can make a party vulnerable to deception; such messages must therefore be viewed with some skepticism. When employing these sources in support of threat identification efforts, pay particular attention to the position and influence wielded by the individual speaker or writer sending a message, how a message coincides with real events, and whether the audience responds favorably or unfavorably to the message itself.

4. **Consider how the basic human needs of each population element are met.** Is the population element of concern relatively autonomous, or is it dependent on someone or something else to fulfill a need? If so, how is the dependency relationship structured? The capability matrix shown above can assist with this step. As stated previously, the dependencies and relationships of a group can produce stresses that can destabilize a situation or help to achieve a new state of stability. Understanding the nature of these relationships and how to exploit them is therefore critical to being able to predict and influence how a relationship will influence events.

5. **Track relationships between relevant population groups identified in IPB step two.** Relevant relationships can be charted in order to determine the interests and intentions of population groups.

Tools currently used by the Army can assist in mapping the relationships between one population element and another. Two of these tools are shown Figure 6.4. A link diagram graphically represents the relationships between population elements. Each of the circles represents individuals; the boxes that surround them indicate their group affiliations. Note that the boxes can represent the name of a group, if known, or an activity in which the individual is known to have participated. This latter mechanism, charting the individual to his known activities, can serve to identify the capabilities and intentions of the various groups to which he belongs.

The association matrix helps to identify the nature of the relationship between individuals or groups. It is a helpful way to identify intelligence requirements about particular people.

RAND*MR1287-6.4*

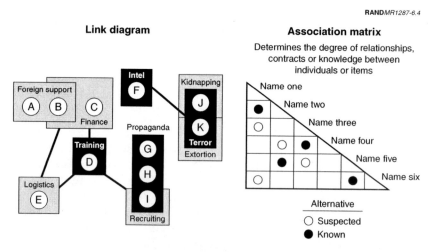

SOURCE: United States Army Intelligence Center and Fort Huachuca, *MOOTW Instructional Materials for the Military Intelligence Officer Transition Course,* Fort Huachuca, AZ: United States Army Intelligence Center and Fort Huachuca, 1999.

Figure 6.4—Relationship Mapping Techniques

Both of these tools provide helpful visualizations of group relationships. Each of them serves as a mechanism for establishing both interest and intent for the population elements involved. These tools can assist in developing questions like: What benefit is "G" gaining from his association with the propaganda element (shown in the link diagram)? What kind of interaction exists between "name five" and "name six" (shown in the association matrix)? These types of questions will hopefully lead the analyst to develop PIR that will establish interest, intent, and possible COAs for each of these groups.

So far, we have sought to characterize population elements in order to place them along a spectrum that helps to define their significance to the operation. This endeavor is critical for noncombat as well as combat operations, for both are likely to contain a variety of population elements. As such, it is an essential component of step three: *identify and evaluate threats and relevant influences*. To define the most threatening elements more completely, it is necessary to evaluate friendly vulnerabilities and how they might be targeted. This is the subject of the next subsection.

> While gaining an objective appreciation for the enemy's capabilities is important, it is equally important to appreciate how the enemy perceives his own capabilities, since it is this image that will have the greatest influence on his actions. The enemy will do what he thinks is possible, not what we think he can do.
>
> MCDP 2
> *Intelligence*

> What [the Russian Army is] able to do under such circumstances, and how it will be done, is quite apparent to other armies, and consequently they can prepare for Western actions. They portray themselves almost exclusively as the attacker and never the defender. Our air operation templates are well known.
>
> Timothy L. Thomas
> *From Grozny to Belgrade: Constructing the*
> *"Mental Toolbox" of Asymmetric Urban Conflict Options*

Friendly vulnerability assessment and reverse IPB. A force itself must determine and evaluate its own vulnerabilities if it is to accurately gauge the viability of threats and exposure to influences posed by others. This task is typically done using an assessment of what the friendly force believes to be its weakest points. A vital task for the intelligence analyst, particularly when conducting IPB, is to "think like the enemy." By seeing the battlefield as the enemy sees it, the intelligence officer can better predict how the adversary will adapt its tactics to a given situation.

Reverse IPB—conducting the four-step intelligence process from the threat's (or other groups along the *continuum of relative interests*) perspective—is a useful and familiar methodology that is invaluable to thorough and comprehensive analysis. This analytic tool enables an intelligence team to think exclusively about how another entity places itself in the context of a situation. This practice can also highlight important differences in situational perception. The S2/G2/J2 should define the operational area from these groups' perspectives when he or she is conducting step one of reverse IPB. The analyst may find that the AO defined by the friendly force is not consistent with how others envision the operation.

Reverse urban terrain analysis can also provide interesting insights. For example, adversaries accustomed to urban fighting involving small-unit tactics may envision battle in a way not contemplated by the friendly force. Rather than looking for wide avenues of approach that they can use while employing fire and maneuver tactics, the adversary might seek safe houses, concealed pathways, or interstructure corridors. Reverse IPB was unwittingly used by the OPFOR during the Marine Corps exercise Project Metropolis held in February 2001. Members of the OPFOR (themselves a company of Marines) knew how the BLUFOR would attempt to enter buildings and maneuver through streets. The OPFOR was therefore able to inflict a significant number of casualties on the BLUFOR by booby-trapping doors and mobility corridors in the most advantageous locations.

The intelligence analyst can use the *capabilities matrix* for the friendly force when conducting step three of reverse IPB. Friendly dependencies and relationships should be scrutinized for real or perceived vulnerabilities. The vulnerabilities that emerge from constructing the matrix from another perspective might often be different from those identified in the friendly force assessment. For instance, the American and British militaries have different force protection measures. Although the United States and the United Kingdom might not see this as a vulnerability, an adversary might view the disparity as a vulnerability that can be exploited. An adversary could, for example, attempt to degrade the relationship between the United States and the United Kingdom by firing on the less protected force, creating a sense of resentment. The adversary might also seek to stir resentment among a city's population by steering it away from thinking that the U.S. soldiers in full "battle rattle" are there to help them.

When constructing COAs for reverse IPB, it is important to do more than simply use courses of action already chosen. It is essential to see the operations as they would be perceived by other parties with the capability, intention, and/or interest to influence the operation. Perception assessment tools, such as the matrices developed in step two and those available from the Army's PSYOP manuals (FM 3-05.3 and FM 33-1-1) can help in this regard. These tools may assist in assuming a position that allows the analyst to see the friendly force from the "outside." Actual U.S. capabilities should be compared to what the other party perceives those capabilities to be. Does the population group or threat believe U.S. capabilities are better than they really are? What are the consequences of misperception? Given this misperception, what does the group or threat think the United States will do? (Note the potential for deception. Both Blue and Red analysts should constantly be looking for Blue deception opportunities during their conduct of the IPB process. Similarly, both should be looking for Red opportunities in this regard so as to better facilitate Blue counterdeception. Further, deception need not be limited to Red groups; others along the *continuum of relative interests* may have reasons for employing it as well.)[10]

Enemy and other COA development should also include the appropriate groups' perspectives regarding friendly HPT, HVT, and NAI given assumptions on expected friendly force COA. Are the HPT and HVT accurate? How can they be protected? Are the NAI correctly placed? Is there a way to use deception to create a false perception at given NAIs?

---

[10]For more information on deception, particularly its uses and benefits in urban operations, see Scott A. Gerwehr and Russell W. Glenn, *The Art of Darkness: Deception and Urban Operations.* Santa Monica, CA: RAND, MR-1132-A, 2000.

Overall, the *continuum of relative interests* and reverse IPB can be valuable tools for identifying the utility and manipulability of each population sector that the friendly force will encounter. They will also help in managing these population sectors as the operation unfolds. Finally, the techniques used to distinguish one population sector from another will help to identify the elements of the population that are most threatening to the friendly force. Once identified, these sectors should undergo the type of threat evaluation that is traditionally a part of IPB.

The next section describes some considerations for the intelligence analyst to employ when assessing urban adversaries or other parties with the capability to influence friendly force actions. Note that the descriptions included are not intended to be an exhaustive compilation. Our intention is to review lessons learned from recent urban engagements in order to spark consideration of how to formally conduct adversary and other influential group evaluation for urban operations. The information included below is drawn primarily from previous urban operations lessons learned, MOUT web pages, and a variety of articles available from the Center for Army Lessons Learned (CALL) and Foreign Military Studies Office (FMSO).

URBAN ADVERSARY AND RELEVANT INFLUENCES EVALUATION

> The asymmetric methods and objectives of an adversary are often far more important than the relative technological imbalance, and the psychological impact of an attack might far outweigh the actual physical damage inflicted. An adversary may pursue an asymmetric advantage on the tactical, operational, or strategic level by identifying key vulnerabilities and devising asymmetric concepts and capabilities to strike or exploit them. To complicate matters, our adversaries may pursue a combination of asymmetries, or the United States may face a number of adversaries who, in combination, create an asymmetric threat.
>
> *Joint Vision 2020*

> Enemy warriors operating in urban areas can engage in a wide variety of asymmetric methods to slow the tempo of military operations, create large numbers of US casualties, and through a variety of barbaric means, attempt to break the will of the American people to continue the fight.

Rather than seeking to achieve victory, the enemy needs only to avoid defeat.

Robert F. Hahn and Bonnie Jezoir
"Urban Warfare and the Urban Warfighter of 2025"

Warriors—what they lack in traditional military organization and equipment they compensate for with tenacity, local knowledge and violence.

ODSCINT
The 21st Century Threat

Professionals are predictable. It's the amateurs that are dangerous.

Murphy's Laws of Combat

Current IPB doctrine covers much of what is known about a "traditional" adversary in force-on-force operations. Interested readers are directed to the various field manuals related to this traditional analysis. The following list, therefore, is heavily weighted toward the urban adversaries that might use nontraditional means to stifle superior U.S. technology, equipment, and personnel. These strategies and tactics, typically labeled "asymmetric," can take a variety of forms; from no-tech and low-tech approaches to high-tech based information warfare campaigns. These adversaries may have no known doctrine. What can be known about them is what can be gained from the lessons-learned literature and recent journalistic accounts of urban battles, some of which is listed in Table 6.1. The table is meant to be illustrative, not comprehensive. It can be used as a starting point in identifying the ways that an adversary might fight in an urban environment.

Clearly, the modern urban adversary does not rely entirely on maneuver warfare to win battles—his technological inferiority and the nature of the terrain do not allow it. This fact makes it very difficult to identify HVT associated with adversary tactics. There may be no key command and control (C2) node to target. Frequently there is no flank against which to advance. The intelligence analyst needs to determine ways to neutralize tactics such as those described in Table 6.1; related HVT and centers of gravity may be as nontraditional as are the tactics themselves.

Table 6.1

Examples of Enemy Urban Warfare Tactics, Strategies, and Weapons

Units tend to be small, somewhat autonomous groups that require limited guidance and intergroup communication.

Decentralization of Chechen command and control created difficulties for the Russians during both battles for Grozny. Chechen groups employed varied and nontraditional tactics, at times deliberately, in other instances because small-unit leaders were adapting to situations they had failed to foresee.[a]

Weapon systems tend to be small and portable.

A typical urban threat arsenal might contain rifles, rocket-propelled grenades (RPGs), and other anti-tank (AT) weapons. Employing such weapons requires little preliminary training or logistical support, but they can be extremely effective. Urban canyons and close quarters make these hand-held weapons all the more effective. Chechen hunter-killer RPG teams were fundamental to neutralizing the Russian armor threat in Grozny.[a]

Commercial off-the-shelf (COTS) technologies are common.

Scanners, mobile TV equipment, jammers, radios, and computers help a less sophisticated force in its efforts to close the technological gap between itself and a regular military organization. Adversaries confronted in Mogadishu, Chechnya, Northern Ireland, Bosnia, and Kosovo all made use of COTS technologies.

Tactics include kidnappings, swarming, raids, ambushes, and the use of snipers, assassinations, and booby traps.

The Provisional Irish Republican Army, Chechens, and Colombian guerillas are all known to have used these tactics. An important element in their employment is the psychological effect they have on the adversary. That an attack can come from any one of five directions—above, below, from the side, front, or behind—increases the degree of mental stress.

Table 6.1—continued

Urban adversaries battle for hearts and minds through the use of information, disinformation, propaganda, and manipulation of the press.

Information operations are increasingly critical to the urban adversary. Because he is striking at the U.S. will to fight, one of the asymmetric adversary's primary methods is to use information warfare tactics. They are relatively cheap and nonlethal. It is generally accepted that Russia lost the information warfare battle during the first Grozny invasion. Media were allowed almost unlimited access to the fighting. As a result, Russian public support for the fighting was low. During the second campaign, media personnel were restricted from entering the operational area and were given stories approved by Russian military or government officials. Domestic support for the Russians was markedly improved as a result.

Thwarting the high-technology assets of a Western force is sought via low-tech or no-tech means.

During the NATO air strikes on Kosovo, the Serbs used corrugated steel to decoy radar and took advantage of dead space and blind spots to defeat reconnaissance satellite collection efforts. Serbs also used smoke to disrupt precision-guided munitions engagements. In Mogadishu, unarmed noncombatants employed kites in attempts to down American helicopters.

The restrictions placed on friendly force activities by treaties, laws of land warfare, and rules of engagement are frequently exploited.

The Chechens positioned a command post in a hospital, demonstrating their disregard for international law.[b] Dropping live power lines over roadways or poisoning water supplies to create panic are other examples of how terror can be used by those who consider themselves unencumbered by Geneva Convention and other standards.

PSYOP, deception, CA, and PA are often employed.

The two battles for Grozny offer considerable anecdotal evidence of PSYOP and deception use. The Chechens altered Russian operations by giving commands in Russian on their enemy's radio nets. Chechens fired from behind the hanging bodies (alive or dead) of Russian soldiers and booby trapped Russian wounded. Carlos Marighella, in his treatise the *Minimanual for the Urban Guerilla,* instructs his readers to undermine the psyche of the more advanced enemy.

Table 6.1—continued

Adversaries use the three-dimensional character of urban terrain to their advantage—operating from all four sides, above, and below.

The Chechens often secured the top floors of buildings in Grozny. Once Russian soldiers entered the building, the Chechens would begin firing through the floor.

Adversaries use the interconnectedness of the city to exploit nodal capabilities.

Yugoslav President Slobodan Milosevic recently demonstrated the power of this capability. "By ingenuity, discreet purchases and some help from its neighbors, Milosevic's government has kept electricity flowing despite NATO's high-tech strikes against distribution grids."[c] In addition, "transnational communities, or diasporas, are taking on new importance. Diasporas provide money, arms, fighters and leaders to their ancestral groups struggling for freedom."[d]

---

[a]For a complete account of the first battle of Grozny, see Timothy L. Thomas, "The Caucasus Conflict and Russian Security: The Russian Armed Forces Confront Chechnya III. The Battle for Grozny, 1–26 January 1995." *Journal of Slavic Military Studies,* March 1997; and Timothy L. Thomas, *Some Asymmetric Lessons of Urban Combat: The Battle of Grozny (1–20 January 1995).* Fort Leavenworth, KS: Foreign Military Studies Office, 1999.

[b]Timothy L. Thomas, *From Grozny to Belgrade: Constructing the "Mental Toolbox" of Asymmetric Urban Conflict Operations,* Fort Leavenworth, KS: Foreign Military Studies Office, 1999.

[c]Edward Cody, "Serbian Struggle Through Standoff With the West," *Washington Post,* February 9, 2000.

[d]Samuel P. Huntington, "A Local Front Of A Global War," *The New York Times,* December 16, 1999.

Tools Used to Assess the Urban Adversary

The USAIC and FH have developed several analytic tools to assist in assessing the interests and intentions of the urban adversary. All of these tools seek to establish a pattern of tactics used by the urban foe. In this regard, they are historical or event-based tools used in efforts to predict events that might follow an established trend. The benefits of these tools are that they can help the intelligence analyst determine the preferred tactics of the adversary, possible motives for his activities, and locations of weapon caches or hide sites. Interests and intentions may perhaps be gauged by careful assessment of who or what has previously been targeted and why. In all cases the analyst can also apply these tools to instances in which the parties being monitored fall into a category other than "adversary."

The incident overlay. Depicts the locations of different adversary actions and types of tactics employed within the AO and AOI. Figure 6.5 is an example. Dr. John Snow's post-event plotting of cholera examples in 1854 London is another example.

Time event chart. Graphically portrays a sequence of events that are believed to create a pattern of activity. In Figure 6.6, a historical analysis of East Timorese troop movements to Dili indicates the presence of particular indicators and warnings regarding these movements. If the analyst makes KOPASSUS an NAI for an East Timorese COA, increased activity spotted there would seem to indicate that troops in Dili will rotate in approximately three months. Other hypotheses are feasible. It is up to the intelligence analyst to further focus his or her collection assets in order to test hypotheses derived using this helpful tool.

RAND*MR1287-6.5*

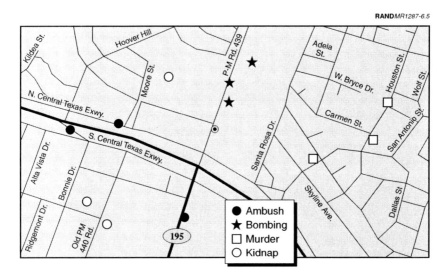

SOURCE: United States Army Intelligence Center and Fort Huachuca, *MOOTW Instructional Materials for the Military Intelligence Officer Transition Course*, Fort Huachuca, AZ: United States Army Intelligence Center and Fort Huachuca, 1999.

Figure 6.5—Incident Overlay

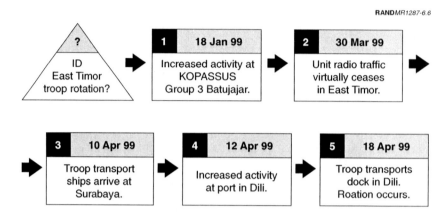

SOURCE: United States Army Intelligence Center and Fort Huachuca, *MOOTW Instructional Materials for the Military Intelligence Officer Transition Course,* Fort Huachuca, AZ: United States Army Intelligence Center and Fort Huachuca, 1999.

Figure 6.6—Time Event Chart

The pattern analysis plot chart. Used to depict the time and date trends of a selected type of activity. The "wagon wheel" represents one month: each concentric circle is a day that is divided into 24 one-hour segments. Events are logged on the wheel as they occur. For instance, in the example shown in Figure 6.7, all bombings take place between four and six in the morning, and all fall on days near the end of the month. Understanding these traits provides the basis for developing hypotheses on the target group's intentions. The timings indicate that the bombers may not seek to kill people; most people are in bed at the hours of detonation. The end of the month could possibly indicate that they are seeking to influence the views of the less wealthy, those whose disgruntlement at having little cash at month's end would make them more likely to support actions that attack establishment targets. Various other hypotheses are feasible. It is up to the intelligence analyst to further focus his or her collection assets in order to test hypotheses derived using this helpful tool.

All three of these tools are well suited for predeployment analysis and for pattern analysis by units deployed in a theater for a long period. However, some situations will preclude their implementation: historical data may not be available, or mission demands may not allow

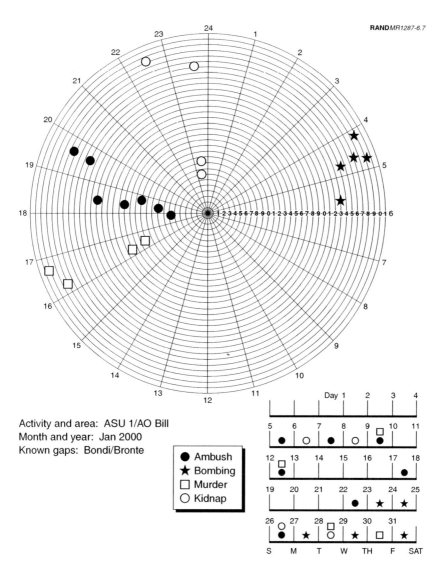

Activity and area: ASU 1/AO Bill
Month and year: Jan 2000
Known gaps: Bondi/Bronte

● Ambush
★ Bombing
□ Murder
○ Kidnap

SOURCE: United States Army Intelligence Center and Fort Huachuca, *MOOTW Instructional Materials for the Military Intelligence Officer Transition Course,* Fort Huachuca, AZ: United States Army Intelligence Center and Fort Huachuca, 1999.

Figure 6.7—Pattern Analysis Plot Chart

the time necessary to compile such data. Another tool, one that can be used independently or in conjunction with those above, is the *capabilities matrix* discussed earlier in this chapter. By assessing the nature of an organization's dependencies, the relationships between its members and those with other groups, and the entity's expressed interests and intentions, it is possible to develop likely group courses of action, the topic of our next chapter.

SUMMARY OF STEP THREE OF IPB FOR URBAN OPERATIONS

The buildings, infrastructure, and people present in urban areas complicate step three of IPB. Perhaps the greatest challenges come in dealing with the number and variety of population groups. The presence of civilians on the battlefield requires the identification of which groups are most threatening and which might otherwise influence friendly forces. The analyst will want to characterize each group using what is known about its capabilities and intentions, and determine how these elements can be used to influence friendly vulnerabilities. The next step is to array population groups along the *continuum of relative interests,* allowing an analysis of which population sectors are most threatening, which might lend assistance, and what approaches are likely to be most successful when dealing with these many demographic elements.

Urban adversaries undergo the same type of analytic scrutiny as would any other type of foe. In addition, mission demands may well require similar, albeit adapted, analyses for groups elsewhere along the *continuum of relative interests.*

Chapter Seven

IPB FOR URBAN OPERATIONS STEP FOUR: DEVELOP NON-U.S. COURSES OF ACTION

It will be vital to identify centers of gravity rapidly and determine the critical vulnerabilities that will be our pathways to them. We won't always have the luxury of a passive foe, and there's no natural law that says that every high-tech war must be fought in a desert with unlimited visibility and good weather.

Carl E. Mundy
Commandant of the U.S. Marine Corps (retired)

Step four of traditional IPB coordinates what is known about the enemy with the limitations and opportunities provided by the terrain and weather. The typical end products of this step are course-of-action descriptions and overlays that depict what the adversary might possibly pursue given the context of the situation. These are products that will ideally reflect how the enemy might maneuver or otherwise operate given specific environmental conditions. The desired goal is to determine how the adversary is likely to behave in a given situation. An additional objective is identification of the target groups' centers of gravity (COG), "the hub[s] of all power and movement, on which everything depends" and means to influence them in the interests of mission accomplishment.[1]

Traditional operations on open terrain against a known enemy made step four of IPB a largely pro forma exercise. Doctrine and tactics were relatively easily mapped onto terrain unrestricted by buildings

---

[1]FM 101-5-1/MCRP 5-2A, *Operational Terms and Graphics*, Washington, D.C.: U.S. Department of the Army, 1997.

and infrastructure. In contrast, urban terrain complicates COA development by restricting maneuver of some units and enhancing the movement opportunities of others. As discussed previously, urban areas also introduce a variety of latent and potential threats that could erode the goals of a mission. All of these potential threats (or possible allies!) need to be considered when developing threat COA for urban IPB. Because of the increased number of real and potential threats, we posit that enemy COA development should be expanded to include each of the population groups identified as part of urban IPB step three while constructing the *continuum of relative interests*. In order to include this idea of expanding COA development beyond an immediately known enemy, we adopt a broader label for urban IPB step four: *develop non-U.S. courses of action.* This step should seek to develop COA for groups that are potential threats, as well as COA for groups that might act together against the United States. COA should also be developed for groups that do not at the outset appear to be threatening but might, because of a series of events, become involved in activities that could impact the overall mission of the unit.

In this chapter we describe methods to assist in developing courses of action and overcoming the additional complexity engendered by a greater number of COA to create. It is important to note that discussion of COA for this chapter is not limited to those for an adversary. Rather, the COA discussed herein include those for all relevant population groups and subgroups identified in IPB step two and categorized in IPB step three.

DEVELOPING NON-U.S. COURSES OF ACTION

> Scientific method is based on the principle of rejecting hypotheses, while tentatively accepting only those hypotheses that cannot be refuted. Intuitive analysis, by comparison, generally concentrates on confirming a hypothesis and commonly accords more weight to evidence supporting a hypothesis than evidence that weakens it.
>
> Richards Heuer
> *The Psychology of Intelligence Analysis*

As demonstrated in the previous chapter, population elements fall along a *continuum of relative interests*. This continuum measures the degree of relative danger and usefulness each population element presents in relation to the successful completion of the friendly mission. The last chapter also introduced the concept that relationships between different population elements can possibly be manipulated based on each element's capabilities to affect another's interests. These ideas are important to keep in mind as we describe COA development for urban IPB.

COA development for urban IPB follows the same procedures as are applicable to traditional IPB. Rather than just consider the enemy, however, COA development considerations must be made for each relevant population group as identified by the *continuum of relative interests.*

> **Identify each population group's desired end state.** Doctrinally, this is conducted only for the known threat; and in combat operations, threat end state is the most critical determination. As much as possible, however, the interests and intentions of each of the population elements identified in step three of urban IPB can help to define the desired end state for each of the identified relevant populations. This information is derived from cultural intelligence, HUMINT, media analysis, and other sources.

> **Work backward, from end state to initiation point, to develop COAs for each non-U.S. actor.** For this step, deriving the capabilities and intentions of each relevant population group will assist in developing COAs and identifying their associated named areas of interest (NAI) and target areas of interest (TAI). The *capabilities matrix* in conjunction with the *relationship matrix* can be used to help build COA for each relevant group. Table 7.1 lists some sample questions to consider when developing these COAs. An additional technique involves analysis of COA that seem unlikely. Start with an assumption that an unexpected event has actually occurred. Then, work backward to explain how this could have happened. This will help develop a list of COA that may not otherwise have been considered.

These techniques can generate COA for each population group. In addition, when evaluating a known adversary for a combat operation, they can be used in conjunction with any analysis of known and supposed tactics of the adversarial force to create enemy COA.

Table 7.1

Sample Questions to Consider When Developing Courses of Action

- Does the population element in question have all of the capabilities required to complete the COA?

- Does the population element have the capability to make the United States or other population elements resident in the AO believe that it can complete the proposed COA?

- Does the population element know of its inherent capability, or is the capability something that can unwittingly affect operations?

- How is each of the capabilities going to be integrated in order to achieve the desired end state?

- Are there several different ways to integrate capabilities to achieve the desired end state?

- What are the interests of the relevant groups? Can they be shaped by the friendly or adversarial force? Have they been shaped already?

- What are the friendly force vulnerabilities? Which population groups are aware of these vulnerabilities?

- What are the known tactics of the adversary?

In addition to traditional COA development practices, we offer a new procedure for urban IPB called the *analysis of competing hypotheses* (ACH). This technique is used to refute COA as they are developed, thus limiting the amount of time spent on unfeasible alternatives. The approach is ideally suited for COA development because it provides inducements to be imaginative and predictive while mitigating the effects of cognitive and analytic shortcomings. It can also be used to systematically evaluate each hypothesized COA. A general discussion of this approach follows. How it is applied to step four of urban IPB comes thereafter.

Analysis of competing hypotheses is an eight-step approach for the evaluation of multiple hypotheses. These steps are listed in Table 7.2.

The list of steps offers nothing new for practiced military intelligence professionals. These steps are conducted repeatedly when developing and analyzing COA. What is new, however, is the systematic and

Table 7.2

Step-by-Step Outline of Analysis of Competing Hypotheses

1. Identify the possible hypotheses [COA] to be considered. Use a group of analysts with different perspectives to brainstorm feasible COA.

2. Make a list of significant evidence and arguments for and against each hypothesis.

3. Prepare a matrix with hypotheses across the top and evidence down the side. Analyze the "diagnosticity" of the evidence and arguments—that is, identify which items are most helpful in judging the relative likelihood of the hypotheses.

4. Refine the matrix. Reconsider the hypotheses and delete evidence and arguments that have no diagnostic value.

5. Draw tentative conclusions about the relative likelihood of each hypothesis. Proceed by trying to disprove the hypotheses rather than prove them.

6. Analyze how sensitive your conclusion is to a few critical items of evidence. Consider the consequences for your analysis if the evidence were wrong, misleading, or subject to a different interpretation.

7. Report conclusions. Discuss the relative likelihood of all the hypotheses, not just the most likely one.

8. Identify milestones for future observation that may indicate events are taking a different course than expected.

SOURCE: Richards Heuer, *The Psychology of Intelligence Analysis*, Washington, D.C.: U.S. Government Printing Office, 1999, p. 97.

conscious application of them to the urban IPB process, as is thinking about the types of analytic pitfalls one might encounter when conducting IPB (such as the us-versus-them mentality, overlooking evaluation of relevant population groups, and the like). The ACH approach may provide the analytic rigor required to evaluate the deluge of information that occurs during urban operations. Three critical components of ACH are particularly helpful in COA development and analysis:

- "Diagnosticity";
- Disproving a hypothesis;

- Evidence sensitivity analysis.

Each one of these elements is discussed briefly below.

> **Diagnosticity.** Diagnosticity is a term used to describe the relative value of a certain piece of evidence. If a piece of evidence seems to support many different hypotheses, it has little diagnostic value. "A common experience is to discover that most of the evidence supporting what you believe is the most likely hypothesis really is not very helpful, because that same evidence is also consistent with other hypotheses."[2]

> **Disproving a hypothesis.** A fundamental precept of the scientific method is to proceed by rejecting or eliminating hypotheses, or at least determining which are unlikely. No matter how much information is consistent with a given hypothesis, one cannot prove that it is true; the same information may also be consistent with one or more other hypotheses. On the other hand, a single item of evidence that is inconsistent with a hypothesis may be sufficient grounds for rejecting that hypothesis.[3]

> **Sensitivity of evidence.** Question the assumptions that drive the outcome of the analysis. "When analysis turns out to be wrong, it is often because of key assumptions that went unchallenged and proved invalid. It is a truism that analysts should identify and question assumptions, but this is much easier said than done. The problem is to determine which assumptions merit questioning. Are there alternate explanations? Are there questionable assumptions? Could the information be incomplete and therefore misleading?"[4] If a COA is too sensitive to one assumption, that assumption will need to be evaluated regularly in order to ensure the value of the hypothesized COA.

By using the three ideas listed above, a proposed COA for any operation can be tested for its value as a distinct, viable COA.

---

[2]Richards Heuer, *The Psychology of Intelligence Analysis,* Washington, D.C.: Center for the Study of Intelligence, Central Intelligence Agency, 1999, p. 102.

[3]Ibid., pp. 103–104.

[4]Ibid., p. 106.

Further Incorporating the Continuum of Relative Interests into COA Development

> The enemy of my enemy is my friend.
>
> *Old proverb*

The *continuum of relative interests* can be used to support the development of friendly and enemy COA, and the COA of groups elsewhere along the continuum. The unique characteristics assigned to each group—determined in the cultural intelligence portion of step two and refined in the determination of interests and capabilities when placing groups into the *continuum of relative interests* in step three—can be used to establish plausible predictions for COA.

In combat operations, the COA developed will primarily be for the friendly and adversarial forces. The COA developed for other population groups identified during steps two and three will seek to determine how the actions taken by the combatants will cause these noncombatants to respond. In MOOTW, the necessity to evaluate each population group's COA will be more critical. Even in these operations, however, to avoid overwhelming the command staff with analysis, it is important to identify the population groups most relevant to the current operation. All other population groups should be kept in mind but need not be at the forefront of analysis.

Each of the population elements arrayed along the continuum will act according to its own interests and intentions. If each group's interests and capabilities are known, the intelligence staff might be able to predict how it will act. It also might be able to determine how one relevant group can influence the actions of another, associated group, wittingly or unwittingly. For instance, in a hypothetical peace enforcement mission, an organized crime group might be classified as an obstacle (as identified on the *continuum of relative interests*) to the friendly force mission during step three because it has the capability to impede unit progress. Its driving interest, however, is to make money rather than interfere with the friendly force. An insurgent group that is intent on disrupting the peace process, identified as adversarial to the friendly force, has the capability to finance this criminal element and does so. The now-mercenary organized crime organization shifts along the continuum to the category of adversary because of its new alliance with the insurgent group. What is important in this assessment, however, is to recall that groups or parts of groups can exist simultaneously in two or more spots along the continuum and that they can change position over time. For instance, if it is believed that the U.S. unit can benefit by co-opting the criminal organization either through greater monetary rewards or some type of coercion, the friendly unit can cause the group to shift along the continuum in a more positive direction. Groups and their relationships should be monitored continually. Addressing this dynamic quality is imperative to creating and maintaining viable COA.

Understanding the relationships between the elements arrayed along the continuum is no less critical than determining where on the continuum each group should appear. For instance, understanding what relationships exist can help to define how an adversary might seek to gain from interactions with allied or sympathetic groups. It may use leverage, coercion, or other means to influence behaviors. The gang cohesion that occurred during the 1992 Los Angeles riots and described in the previous chapter is an example of how rival groups used negotiation to achieve their overarching goal. A similar situation arose in Mogadishu in 1993. While opposing clans did not always form formal pacts, they did tend to turn against the foreign presence represented by the United States and its fellow coalition members, focusing violence against these new targets rather than each other.

Analyzing the Higher-Order Effects

COA development too rarely considers how activities—friendly force, enemy, or noncombatant—might produce unintended consequences. The likelihood of such second- and higher-order effects are of notable concern in urban environments. The increased density of individuals, infrastructure, and buildings means that a given action is more likely to have unintended consequences; further, those consequences will be more widely felt and their impact will spread in less time than in other environments. For instance, a broken sewer pipe or chemical spill in the middle of town can immediately disrupt traffic flow over several square kilometers and threaten an outbreak of disease or other problems rapidly spread by citizens or contaminated materials moving about the city. Spillage of the waste can poison the water supply, relied upon by thousands or tens of thousands within a few kilometers of the spill. A military force manned with engineer, transport, and medical personnel sufficient only to care for its own soldiers could find itself quickly overwhelmed by the need to repair the break, coordinate delivery of fresh water, and treat those who might have been affected.

Determining the higher-order effects of an activity is not unlike assessing the reactions of population groups. It involves an evaluation of the interconnectedness of relevant factors and how interactions can cause unintended outcomes. The *capabilities matrix* introduced in the previous chapter can assist in determining the relationships that exist in the operational area. There are also several technologies that can help predict the spread of disease or airborne agents that are currently being used by disaster relief agencies and intelligence organizations. These technologies, while useful, do not take into consideration all of the possible consequences that can be imagined.

An example of several immediate and lasting higher-order effects can be gleaned from the NATO bombing of Kosovo in 2000. Almost immediately, Kosovo suffered a refugee problem when Serbs reacted by purging entire areas of Albanian residents. This migration had the second-order effect of complicating NATO targeting, for the Serbs used the refugees as cover by positioning them close to their own forces, deliberately putting them at risk should NATO aircraft engage the legitimate targets. Further, at the operational and strategic levels, the massive population displacement created shelter and sustenance shortfalls in Albania, requiring delays in the delivery of military supplies so that tents, food, and other aid could be provided to refugee camps.

In short, COA development for step four of urban IPB will normally involve far more than evaluation of a single adversary. COAs for all population elements should be considered, prioritized, and incorporated into the process to adequately assess all effects on any type of operation. They must thereafter be continuously monitored and updated to reflect changes in the environment, group dynamics, or interrelationships. IPB step four for urban contingencies expands the scope of traditional IPB to assimilate all relationships and interconnections that exist in an urban operational area.

Chapter Eight

RECOMMENDATIONS

As discussed throughout the text, cities contain buildings, infrastructure, and people that affect all types of military operations and their associated intelligence efforts. Indeed, the quantity and complexity of urban areas simultaneously degrade and enhance mission and intelligence undertakings. The effects of media reportage provide a good example of this duality. Information reported from Mogadishu influenced the termination of U.S. military operations in Somalia. Conversely, the same type of television reporting has been used as a real-time intelligence source during Operation Desert Storm and other contingencies. **The volume and density of additional components that can affect operational outcomes require a method of analysis that is flexible and thorough enough to accommodate them. The IPB process is well suited for this purpose. What is necessary is for IPB tools and techniques to be adapted to undertake urban complexities in a manner to assure that the vast amount of information is organized and analyzed in a way that avoids overwhelming the intelligence and command staffs.** This report has identified existing IPB methods and tools and introduced new ideas that can help analysts meet this requirement.

RECOMMENDATIONS

- IPB is a sound methodology for assessing the difficult operational and intelligence challenges of urban operations.

- IPB tools, techniques, and assumptions need to be augmented and modified to accommodate the additional complexities posed by urbanized terrain.

This review of the methods currently used and the introduction of additional procedures offers analysts several concepts for improving IPB to better serve them during urban operations. These concepts include the following:

- **Population analysis, which includes both demographic analysis and cultural intelligence, should come to the analytic foreground.** Current IPB doctrine focuses on determining a city's layout and construction. Population analysis is included as part of the "other" category in current doctrine. The prevalence of people in urban areas and the many ways they can affect operations, including how population groups can hinder threat identification and evaluation, suggests that the population should receive far greater attention.

- **Population analysis should seek to identify the characteristics of each population group and subgroup to determine how it will act and interact within the area of operations and associated area of interest.** As part of this effort, commanders and their intelligence staffs should attempt to map the "population terrain" of the deployment area. The demographic analysis and cultural intelligence products listed and referenced herein will assist the unit in conducting ground as well as information operations. This analysis will also help the unit determine potential secondary effects and predict less obvious effects attributable to the unit's actions.

- **The role of media and information operations and the tools, audiences, and messages needed for properly integrating them into plans and operations should receive more attention when conducting IPB.** The media is often cited as having a role (sometimes a mission-altering one) in MOUT. Understanding how the military can affect and be affected by information can be a critical component of urban operation success. If understood and used correctly, it could also be used as a nonlethal means to influence mission outcomes. IPB should therefore more thoroughly address both media and information operations.

- **The perceptions of each of the population groups should be understood.** Understanding that different population groups perceive the same events in different ways is important during any type of operation. Those groups may interpret events and friendly force actions unexpectedly. This is perhaps more critical in urban settings due to the number and density of population groups and the prevalence of mass media.

- **Threats and other influences should be clearly defined and identified based on each population group's interests, intentions, and capabilities and the vulnerabilities of the friendly force.** Current doctrine does not have a definition of threat. Rather, doctrine is based on Cold War paradigms and Soviet style threat models. The population groups along with their essential needs and interests (such as a lack of fresh water) that most threaten or might otherwise influence mission accomplishment should be more effectively identified and evaluated.

- **The relationships and interconnectivity between population elements, infrastructure, buildings, and the underlying terrain are significant and worth investigating.** Current doctrine, other than that for intelligence support for SASO, lacks guidance on how to evaluate the relationships among these four elements. The immediate and follow-on effects of this interconnectivity (e.g., the repercussions of an inoperable power substation could include public outcry, death, or disease) are not included in current doctrine. Because of the way the components of a city interact, it is suggested that these relationships and interconnectivities be better evaluated in order to more thoroughly address possible outcomes of friendly, enemy, and noncombatant courses of action.

- **A comprehensive set of urban adversary tactics should be compiled in order to reduce the vulnerability of the friendly force to surprise.** Currently, the U.S. Army does not have a comprehensive set of tactics that are typically used by combatants in urban areas. It would be useful if such a compilation existed in order for deployed units to predict adversary COA.

- **COA development should include all relevant population groups and effects that reach beyond the typical action-reaction-counteraction approach to wargaming.** It has been noted throughout the text that the presence of uniquely urban features—people, construction, infrastructure—creates ripple effects that are less influential in other types of terrain. As a result, alternatives should include not only the factors included in traditionally constructed friendly and adversary COA. They should also include the effects COA will have on other components of the urban AO, AOI, and battlespace. Depending on mission needs, independent COA should also be developed for each relevant population group.

URBAN AUGMENTATIONS TO CURRENT IPB DOCTRINE

This report has set out to address the intelligence dilemmas and opportunities presented by a city by introducing some techniques and ideas to focus intelligence efforts and manage their complexity. As stated throughout the text, many of the tools and techniques listed herein are already a part of the command and intelligence staff analytic toolkit. These extant tools are not listed here. Rather, we list only the new instruments proposed to augment current doctrine. Each of these is suggested as an addition to the current toolkit. They can be used independently or together, depending on the needs of the commander and the task at hand. Also worth reiterating is that it is not expected that each of these tools should be used for every operation by every unit. Some units simply lack the resources to complete the recommended analyses. Some missions might not warrant undertaking an analysis of all population groups. The tools listed here and throughout the text are offered as suggestions and are meant to stimulate thought on how to address the several challenges created by urbanized terrain.

- **Population OCOKA.** Uses the familiar mnemonic of terrain analysis to assess the effects of a city's population on the full range of military operations.

- **Media analysis.** A discussion similar to that found in current PSYOP doctrine of how to investigate the means, sources, target audience, and messages of media reportage.

- **Non-U.S. actor analysis.** A discussion of the actors to be considered and characterized in order to work more effectively in an urban environment. The actors include members of a coalition force, international aid organizations, civilians on the battlefield, and international audiences.

- **Perception assessment matrices.** A tool to help the intelligence analyst understand how members of various population groups view events and other groups.

- **Threat identification.** That current doctrine does not define "threat" presents a variety of potential analytic pitfalls. In the text we provide a specific definition that can be used to characterize each population subgroup based on its interests, intentions, and capabilities. An adversary is defined in this work as an element of the population that has some current capability and intention to negatively influence mission accomplishment by exploiting a friendly vulnerability. It is noted that each population group can be evaluated based on its capabilities, interests, and intentions in order to determine whether it can threaten a unit's mission or benefit it.

  — **Capabilities matrix.** A tool used to compile and compare the capabilities of each relevant population group. Used as part of threat and other influence identification and evaluation, the data collected for the matrix can help establish salient relationships between population groups or between population groups and the infrastructure.

  — **Interest and intent assessment.** Methods are proposed for deciphering population group interests and intents.

- **Continuum of relative interests.** A tool to help visualize the relationship of each population group with others. It is also used to evaluate a particular group in terms of its capabilities, interests, and intentions. When used along with an assessment of the friendly unit's vulnerabilities, it is also a way of understanding how each population group within the AO and associated AOI and battlespace can be perceived as enabling or obstructing the mission, and, in turn, how each might be used or shaped to ensure mission success.

- **Analysis of competing hypotheses.** This tool is not new to intelligence efforts. Rather, it is a technique used by many in intelligence organizations as a method for determining the most realistic course of action. It is presented here because it is not currently part of IPB doctrine.

Along with these specific recommendations, we suggest three additional general modifications of IPB doctrine and practice.

- An automated system should be developed to help manage all of the information required to conduct MOUT IPB analysis. Automated systems can be used to organize data, prioritize intelligence requirements, and develop situational awareness in the service of compiling realistic COA.

- Additional instruction on analytical approaches should be included in the USAIC and FH curriculum. Instruction currently includes coverage of written doctrine, but guidance is lacking on methods of approaching, conceiving, or solving complex problems. Further instruction on analytic thinking and problem solving is recommended.

- There is a need for improved predeployment urban intelligence gathering. This should include investigation of a city's layout, building construction, and demographic and cultural intelligence.

IPB provides an excellent framework for organizing data and managing information collection. It is flexible and robust enough to handle the complex challenges posed by today's villages, towns, and cities. However, adaptation is necessary if the process is to be an effective, efficient tool for planning and executing urban operations.

WEB SITES FOR CONDUCTING URBAN IPB

AMERICAN EXPRESS VIRTUAL TOURS

*http://travel.americanexpress.com/travel/personal/resources/ipix/
destin.asp*

Provides 360-degree views of famous locations in world cities.

BRITANNICA ONLINE WORLD PAGES

http://www.britannica.com/bcom/world/0,5758,,00.html

Provides background on the history, culture, and economics of a
country or city, as well as direct links to "best of the web" sources
of a particular aspect of the city or culture. The encyclopedia can
also be used to review the prevalent social aspects of a particular
culture more deeply. Few pictures of relevant structures may be
found on the web pages.

CIA WORLD FACTBOOK

http://www.odci.gov/cia/publications/factbook/index.html

Provides general information at the country level.

THE EMBASSY PAGE

http://www.embpage.org/

Embassy and consular information is included along with a comprehensive list of newspaper hotlinks.

EXCITE TRAVEL PAGE

http://www.excite.com/travel/

Travel guides, including descriptions of world cuisine and customs.

INTERNET RESOURCES FOR TEACHING GLOBAL STUDIES

http://www.westga.edu/~econ/global.html

An excellent collection of both academic and industry sources providing insights into any world destination.

JOURNAL OF GEO-POLITICS

http://FowlerLibrary.com/Kiosk/

Provides historical sources for many cities and countries around the world. It also has many links to other news and information sources.

LIBRARY OF CONGRESS COUNTRY STUDIES HANDBOOK

http://lcweb2.loc.gov/frd/cs/cshome.html

Provides good background information on the history and societies of countries.

LONELY PLANET COUNTRY SEARCH PAGE

http://www.lonelyplanet.com/dest/

Gives general information about any region. Includes information on economy, culture, and weather.

PREVIEW TRAVEL PHOTO GUIDE

http://destinations.previewtravel.com/DestGuides/PhotoWorld/ 1,1858,WEB,00.html

Provides still photos and slide shows of common activities occurring in prominent world cities. Images generally include culturally significant structures in a city.

PREVIEW TRAVEL VIDEO GUIDE

*http://destinations.previewtravel.com/DestGuides/VideoWorld/
0,1348,WEB,00.html*

Provides 360-degree visual imagery of frequently traveled world areas. Although the site does not include a wide variety of cities to which U.S. forces may be deployed, the technology used for this site could be valuable to U.S. forces.

RELIEF WEB

http://www.reliefweb.int

Although compiled to assist aid organizations, the maps and graphics provided are excellent sources of demographic information, historical descriptions of events, refugee status, and relevant infrastructure status.

YAHOOLIGANS COUNTRIES OF THE WORLD

http://www.yahooligans.com/Around_the_World/Countries/

Arguably, the best site for quick-reference materials and well-organized links to more in-depth analysis of global locales.

ARTICLES

Arkin, William M. "Smart Bombs, Dumb Targeting?" *Bulletin of the Atomic Scientists*, May–June 2000: 46–48.

Bulloch, Gavin. "Military Doctrine and Counterinsurgency: A British Perspective." *Parameters*, Summer 1996: 4–16.

Cody, Edward. "Serbian Struggle Through Standoff With the West." *Washington Post*, 9 February 2000.

Erlanger, Steven. "Torn Mitrovica Reflects West's Trials in Kosovo." *The New York Times*, 27 February 2000.

Gall, Carlotta. "Shock of Kosovo Violence May Prove Incentive for Peace." *The New York Times*, 18 February 2000.

Glenn, Russell W. "Fox Trot: Seeking Preparedness for Military Urban Operations." *Armed Forces Journal International*, May 1999: 46–49.

Gordon, Michael R. "In Occupied Chechnya, Order Comes Without Allegiance." *The New York Times*, 22 November 1999.

Grau, Lester W., and Jacob W. Kipp. "Urban Combat: Confronting the Specter." *Military Review*, July–August 1999: 9–17.

Hahn, Robert F., and Bonnie Jezior. "Urban Warfare and the Urban Warfighter of 2025." *Parameters*, Summer 1999: 74–86.

Herz, J.C. "Game Theory: At Play, It Takes the Army to Save a Village." *The New York Times*, 3 February 2000.

House, John M. "The Enemy After Next." *Military Review*, March–April 1998: 22–28.

Huntington, Samuel P. "A Local Front Of A Global War." *The New York Times*, 16 December 1999.

Madan, Lieutenant General Vijay. "Population Terrain: The Neglected Factor of Counter-Insurgency Operations." *Indian Defense Review*, Vol. 12, No. 2, April–June 1997.

Murphy, Kim. "Anarchists Deployed New Tactics in Violent Seattle Demonstrations." *Los Angeles Times*, 16 December 1999.

Peters, Ralph. "The Human Terrain of Urban Operations." *Parameters*, Spring 2000: 4–12.

Peters, Ralph. "Our Soldiers, Their Cities." *Parameters*, Spring 1996: 43–50.

Priest, Dana. "Waging Peace in Kosovo: Mission Forces U.S. Soldiers to Adapt to Civilian Tasks." *Washington Post*, 23 November 1999.

Scalard, Douglas. "People of Whom We Know Nothing: When Doctrine Isn't Enough." *Military Review*, July–August 1997.

Stech, Frank J. "Winning the CNN Wars." *Parameters*, Autumn 1994: 37–56.

Steele, Robert D., and Mark M. Lowenthal. "Open Source Intelligence: Private Sector Capabilities to Support DoD Policy, Acquisitions, and Operations." *Defense Daily Network Special Report,*. 5 May 1998.

Thomas, Timothy L. "The Battle for Grozny: Deadly Classroom for Urban Combat." *Parameters*, Summer 1999: 87–102.

Thomas, Timothy L. "The Caucasus Conflict and Russian Security: The Russian Armed Forces Confront Chechnya III. The Battle for Grozny, 1–26 January 1995." *Journal of Slavic Military Studies*, March 1997: 50–108.

BOOKS

Alexander, John B. *Future War: Non-Lethal Weapons in Twenty-First Century Warfare.* New York: St. Martin's Press, 1999.

Allen, Charles. *The Savage Wars of Peace: Soldiers' Voices 1945–1989.* London: Michael Joseph, 1990.

Bowden, Mark. *Black Hawk Down: A Story of Modern War.* New York: Atlantic Monthly Press, 1999.

Burleson, Willard M. *Mission Analysis During Future Military Operations on Urbanized Terrain.* Fort Leavenworth, KS: U.S. Army and General Staff College, June 2000.

Chuikov, Vasili I. *The Battle for Stalingrad.* New York: Holt Rinehart and Winston, 1964.

Cronon, William. *Nature's Metropolis: Chicago and the Great West.* New York: W.W. Norton and Company, 1991.

Delk, James D. *Fires and Furies: The Los Angeles Riots of 1992.* Palm Springs, CA: ETC Publications, 1995.

D'este, Carlo. *Bitter Victory: The Battle for Sicily 1943.* Glasgow: William Collins Sons and Co. Ltd, 1988.

Dupuy, R. Ernest, and Trevor N. Dupuy. *The Encyclopedia of Military History: From 3500 B.C. to the Present.* San Francisco: Harper and Row, 1977.

Edwards, Sean J.A. *Freeing Mercury's Wings: Improving Tactical Communications in Cities.* Santa Monica, CA: RAND, MR-1316-A, 2001.

Edwards, Sean J.A. *Mars Unmasked: The Changing Face of Urban Operations.* Santa Monica, CA: RAND, MR-1173-A, 2000.

Friedman, Thomas L. *From Beirut to Jerusalem.* New York: Farrar, Strauss and Giroux, 1989.

Gerwehr, Scott, and Russell W. Glenn. *The Art of Darkness: Deception and Urban Operations.* Santa Monica, CA: RAND, MR-1132-A, 2000.

Glenn, Russell W. *Combat in Hell.* Santa Monica, CA: RAND, MR-780-A/DARPA, 1996.

Glenn, Russell W., et al. *Denying the Widowmaker: Summary of Proceedings.* Santa Monica, CA: RAND, CF-143-A, 1998.

Glenn, Russell W. *Heavy Matter: Urban Operations' Density of Challenges.* Santa Monica, CA: RAND, MR-1239-JS/A, 2000.

Glenn, Russell W. *Marching Under Darkening Skies.* Santa Monica, CA: RAND, MR-1007-A, 1999.

Glenn, Russell W. *"...We Band of Brothers": the Call for Joint Urban Operations Doctrine.* Santa Monica, CA: RAND, DB-270-JS/A, 1998.

Hammel, Eric. *The Root: The Marines in Beirut, August 1982– February 1984.* San Diego: Harcourt Brace Jovanovich, 1985.

Heuer, Richards J. *The Psychology of Intelligence Analysis.* Washington, D.C.: Center for the Study of Intelligence, Central Intelligence Agency, 1999.

Spiller, Roger J. *Sharp Corners: Urban Operations at Century's End.* Fort Leavenworth, KS: Combat Studies Institute, 2000.

Tellis, Ashley J., Thomas S. Szayna, and James A. Winnefeld. *Anticipating Ethnic Conflict.* Santa Monica, CA: RAND, 1997.

Wentz, Larry K. (ed). *Lessons from Bosnia: The IFOR Experience.* Vienna, VA: CCRP, 1997.

MILITARY AND TECHNICAL REPORTS

British Army Field Manual. *Operations in Specific Environments: Urban Operations.* London: Ministry of Defence, 1999.

CALL Newsletter No. 96-12, Intelligence Preparation of the Battlefield. Fort Leavenworth, KS: Center for Army Lessons Learned, 17 January 1997.

Caniano, William M. *Uncertainty, Intelligence and IPB: The Role of the Intelligence Officer in Shaping and Synchronizing the Opera-*

tional Battlefield. Newport, RI: College of Naval Command and Staff, 1992.

Ellefson, Richard A. *Urban Terrain Zone Characteristics.* Aberdeen Proving Ground, MD: U.S. Army Engineering Laboratory, 1987.

Field Manual 3-05.3, *Psychological Operations.* Washington, D.C.: Department of the Army, 2000.

Field Manual 5-33, *Terrain Analysis.* Washington, D.C.: Department of the Army, July 1998.

Field Manual 100-5, *Operations.* Washington, D.C.: Department of the Army, 1993.

Field Manual 19-15, *Civil Disturbances.* Washington, D.C.: Department of the Army, 1995.

Field Manual 33-1-1, *Psychological Operations Techniques and Procedures.* Washington, D.C.: Department of the Army, 1994.

Field Manual 34-3, *Intelligence Analysis.* Washington, D.C.: Department of the Army, 1990.

Field Manual 34-7, *IEW Support for Stability Operations and Support Operations (Initial Draft).* Fort Huachuca, AZ: U.S. Army Intelligence Center and Fort Huachuca, 1999.

Field Manual 34-8, *Commander's Handbook on Intelligence.* Washington, D.C.: Department of the Army, 1992.

Field Manual 34-8-2, *Intelligence Officers Handbook.* Washington, D.C.: Department of the Army, 1998.

Field Manual 34-130, *Intelligence Preparation of the Battlefield.* Washington, D.C.: Department of the Army, 1994.

Field Manual 34-130/MCRP 2-12A, *Intelligence Preparation of the Battlefield (Initial Draft).* Washington, D.C.: Department of the Army, 1999.

Field Manual 34-130/MCRP 2-12A, *Intelligence Preparation of the Battlefield (Coordinating Draft).* Fort Huachuca, AZ: U.S. Army Intelligence Center and Fort Huachuca, 1999.

Field Manual 90-10, *Military Operations on Urbanized Terrain (MOUT)*. Washington, D.C.: Department of the Army, 1979.

Field Manual 90-10-1, *An Infantryman's Guide to Urban Combat*. Washington, D.C.: Department of the Army, 1982.

Field Manual 101-5-1/MCRP 5-2A, *Operational Terms and Graphics*. Washington, D.C.: Department of the Army and U.S. Marine Corps, September 30, 1997.

Grau, Lester. *Urban Warfare Communications: A Contemporary Russian View*. Fort Leavenworth, KS: Foreign Military Studies Office, 1996.

Grimsley, William F. *Intelligence Preparation of the Future Operational Battlefield*. Fort Leavenworth, KS: School of Advanced Military Studies and General Staff College, 1994.

James, William T., Jr. *From Seige to Surgical: The Evolution of Urban Combat From World War II to the Present and Its Effect on Current Doctrine*. Fort Leavenworth, KS: U.S. Army Command and General Staff College, 1998.

Johnson, Richard. *Learning Unfamiliar Ground: Terrain Knowledge for Contingency Operations*. Carlisle Barracks, PA: U.S. Army War College, 1992.

Joint Publication 1-02, *Department of Defense Dictionary of Military and Associated Terms*. Washington, D.C.: Office of the Chairman, The Joint Chiefs of Staff, March 23, 1994, as amended through April 6, 1999,

Joint Publication 2-01. *Joint Intelligence Support to Military Operations*. Washington, D.C.: U.S. Joint Chiefs of Staff, 20 November 1996.

Joint Publication 2-01.3. *Joint Tactics, Techniques and Procedures for Joint Intelligence Preparation of the Battlespace (Preliminary Coordinating Draft)*. Washington, D.C.: U.S. Joint Chiefs of Staff, 9 July 1999.

Joint Publication 3-0. *Doctrine for Joint Operations*. Washington, D.C.: U.S. Joint Chiefs of Staff, 2001.

Joint Publication 3-07. *Joint Doctrine for Military Operations Other Than War*. Washington, D.C.: U.S. Joint Chiefs of Staff, 16 June 1995.

Marine Corps Intelligence Activity. *Generic Information Requirements Handbook*. MCIA-1540-002-95, Quantico, VA: United States Marine Corps, 1995.

Marine Corps Intelligence Activity. *The Urban Century: Developing World Urban Trends and Possible Factors Affecting Military Operations*. MCIA-1586-003-9, Quantico, VA: United States Marine Corps, 1997.

Marine Corps Intelligence Activity. *Urban Generic Information Requirements Handbook (GIRH)*. MCIA-1586-005-99. Quantico, VA: United States Marine Corps, 1998.

Marine Corps Doctrinal Publication 2, *Intelligence*. Washington, D.C.: Department of the Navy, 1997.

Marine Corps Warfighting Publication 2-1, *Intelligence Operations*. Washington, D.C.: Department of the Navy, 1996.

Marine Corps Warfighting Publication 3-35.3, *Military Operations on Urbanized Terrain (MOUT)*. Washington, D.C.: Department of the Navy, 1998.

Marks, James A. *In Search of the Center of Gravity: Operational Intelligence Preparation of the Battlefield*. Fort Leavenworth, KS: School of Advanced Military Studies and General Staff College, 1990.

Megill, Todd A. *Terrain and Intelligence Collection*. Fort Leavenworth, KS: School of Advanced Military Studies and General Staff College, 1996.

Moss, Robert. *Urban Guerilla Warfare*. Aldephi Paper number seventy-nine. London: The International Institute for Strategic Studies, 1971.

Phelps, Ruth H. *Intelligence Preparation of the Battlefield: Critique and Recommendations*. Alexandria, VA: U.S. Army Research Institute for the Behavioral and Social Sciences, 1984.

Phelps, Ruth H., Judith A. Enlert, and Sharon A. Mutter. *Application of a Cognitive Model for Army Training: Handbook for Strategic Intelligence Analysis.* Technical Report 654. Alexandria, VA: U.S. Army Research Institute for the Behavioral and Social Sciences, 1984.

Pogue, Forrest C. *United States Army in World War II: European Theater of Operations, the Supreme Command.* Washington D.C.: Department of the Army, 1954.

Purcell, Thomas C. *Operational Level Intelligence: Intelligence Preparation of the Battlefield.* Carlisle Barracks, PA: U.S. Army War College, 1989.

Rodriguez, Guillermo A. *Intelligence Preparation of the Battlefield: Is It Worth the Effort?* Fort Leavenworth, KS: School of Advanced Military Studies and General Staff College, 1991.

Thaden, Russell H. *Intelligence Preparation of the Battlefield and Predictive Intelligence.* Fort Leavenworth, KS: School of Advanced Military Studies and General Staff College, 1986.

Thomas, Timothy L. *From Grozny to Belgrade: Constructing the "Mental Toolbox" of Asymmetric Urban Conflict Options.* Fort Leavenworth, KS: Foreign Military Studies Office, October 1999.

Thomas, Timothy L. *Some Asymmetric Lessons of Urban Combat: The Battle of Grozny (1–20 January 1995).* Fort Leavenworth, KS: Foreign Military Studies Office, 1999.

Urban Combat Operations: Tactics, Techniques and Procedures (Coordinating Draft). Fort Leavenworth, KS: Center for Army Lessons Learned, 1999. *ftp://mout:draft@callftp.army.mil*

Urban Warfare: The Insights of Other Nations. Cultural Intelligence Seminar, Summary Report. Quantico, VA: Marine Corps Combat Development Command, 22 May 1997.

WEB SITES

Abdullaev, Nabi. "New Rebel Tactics Ambush Russians; Trench Warfare Gives Way to Hit-and-Run Guerrilla Raids." *http://www.Msnbc.com.*

Barth, Fritz J. "The Urban Awareness Concept."
The MOUT Homepage.
http://www.geocities.com/Pentagon/6453/urbanawareness.html.

Dilegge, David P. "Urban Analysis—A Need at All Levels of Operation
and Command: And Particularly for Marine Expeditionary
Forces."
The MOUT Homepage.
www.geocities.com/Pentagon/6453/uaca.html.

Grau, Lester. "Changing Russian Urban Tactics: The Aftermath of
the Battle for Grozny." *INSS Strategic Forum,* July 1995.
http://call.army.mil/call/fmso/fmsopubs/issues/grozny.htm.

Urban Intelligence Preparation of the Battlefield (IPB): Considera-
tions and Issues. 1st Marine Division MOUT Intelligence
Conference 7 January 1999.
http://www.geocities.com/Pentagon/6453.

White, Jeffrey B. "A Different Kind of Threat: Some Thoughts on
Irregular Warfare."
http://www.odci.gov/csi/studies/96unclas/iregular.htm.